Riding Out
A guide to hacking and trekking

Supporting you through every stage

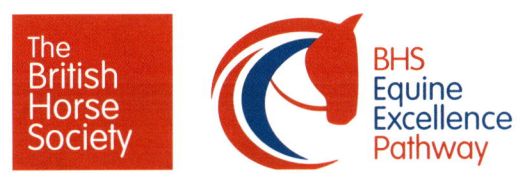

Riding Out
A guide to hacking and trekking

KENILWORTH PRESS

Copyright © 2019 The British Horse Society

First published in the UK in 2019 by Kenilworth Press,
an imprint of Quiller Publishing Ltd

British Library Cataloguing-in-Publication Data
A catalogue record for this book is available from the British Library

ISBN 978 1 910016 35 0

The right of The British Horse Society to be identified as the author of this work has been asserted in accordance with the Copyright, Design and Patent Act 1988.

The information in this book is true and complete to the best of our knowledge. All recommendations are made without any guarantee on the part of the Publisher, who also disclaims any liability incurred in connection with the use of this data or specific details.

All rights reserved. No part of this book may be reproduced or transmitted in any form or by any means, electronic or mechanical including photocopying, recording or by any information storage and retrieval system, without permission from the Publisher in writing.

Edited by Martin Diggle

Printed in Great Britain by Bell and Bain Ltd, Glasgow

Kenilworth Press

An imprint of Quiller Publishing Ltd
Wykey House, Wykey, Shrewsbury SY4 1JA
Tel: 01939 261616
Email: info@quillerbooks.com
Website: www.kenilworthpress.co.uk

Contents

Preface 6

Acknowledgements 6

Introduction 7

SECTION 1   ROLES AND RESPONSIBLITIES OF RIDE HELPERS, RIDE LEADERS AND OWNERS AND MANAGERS OF RIDING CENTRES 17

    Chapter 1   Roles and Responsiblities of a Ride Helper 19

    Chapter 2   Roles and Responsibilities of a Stage 2 Ride Leader 29

    Chapter 3   Roles and Responsibilities of a Stage 3 Trail Leader 37

    Chapter 4   Legislation 53

SECTION 2   PREPARATION AND KNOWLEDGE REQUIRED TO FACILITATE RIDING OUT 67

    Chapter 5   Training and Fittening Horses for Riding Out 69

    Chapter 6   Allocating Horses to Riders 81

    Chapter 7   Useful Skills and Knowledge for Planning Rides 97

SECTION 3   RIDING OUT IN PRACTICE 125

    Chapter 8   Leading a Ride Out 127

    Chapter 9   Planning and Leading Longer Rides 157

    Chapter 10   Caring for Horses on Return from a Ride 165

SECTION 4   ONGOING TRAINING AND DEVELOPMENT 171

    Chapter 11   Staff Training and Development 173

What's Next? 183

Preface

The opportunities to gain experience, and the value of professional qualifications, will be appreciated by a raft of people from those seeking seasonal work in trekking centres, career-orientated trek leaders or indeed from those wishing to run their own establishment that offers riding out at any level. This book is aimed to support and inform all these individuals and equip them with the tools to progress. By definition this will include information regarding the necessary legislation and guidelines involved in running a centre where riding outside of an arena is part of what is on offer. If you currently have a basic level of skill and knowledge within the equestrian industry and wish to work in the equestrian tourism sector, and thus to enhance your knowledge and gain a qualification within that sector, or if you are an aspiring centre manager and plan on running an equestrian business in the future, you will find information and guidance to help you within these pages.

The information herein will also be valuable to people who wish to take part as clients on escorted hacks or longer rides out and, indeed, to those who enjoy riding out as private owners.

Acknowledgements

The British Horse Society acknowledges with thanks the following individuals who provided assistance with the text; Cindy Russell, Pauline Brimson, Candy Cameron, Anthony Eddies-Davies and Sarah Spencer-Williams.

The British Horse Society also acknowledges with thanks the assistance of the following riding centres and their staff in the production of the photographs for this book; Wellington Riding Ltd and Castle Leslie Equestrian Centre. Pictures throughout this publication are supplied by Parkway and Jon Stroud Photography.

Introduction

Benefits of hacking for horses

Benefits of hacking for riders

Potential economic and business benefits

Introduction

The popularity of the horse in the United Kingdom has continued to grow year on year since the successes at the London Olympics in 2012. This has brought equestrian sport to the forefront in the nation's mind, to be reinforced in more recent years by Nick Skelton's showjumping gold medal at Rio in 2016, the wide-ranging achievements in dressage of Charlotte Dujardin and Valegro and the British eventing teams' individual and team gold medals at the 2018 World Equestrian Games. Equestrianism is an extremely popular and healthy activity for people of all ages, partly because it is a diverse, family-friendly sport that men and women can enjoy on an equal footing. The equestrian industry includes anything and everything to do with horses and ponies and associated businesses include; riding schools, livery yards, competition yards, trekking centres, breeders, trainers, welfare charities and also veterinary and other therapeutic services, equine dental technicians, farriers and feed merchants, tack and clothing manufacturers, shows and event services. Leisure riding is the most common equestrian pursuit, although riding lessons and competing at the lower levels are also on the increase. That said, an increasing number of people who ride in riding schools look forward to going out for a hack as a change from having lessons in the arena.

People on holiday also tend to try riding out for a short hack as part of seeing the countryside, and surveys have shown that getting out in the fresh air is good for your head, heart and

Hacking across open countryside.

body. A study conducted by the University of Derby in 2016 showed that spending more time interacting with nature and being in natural environments significantly boosted people's health and happiness. Hacking is a great way for family and friends to catch up and it works wonders for those who are not very confident in the saddle.

Riding outside of an arena or competition environment is a pleasure that is available to riders of all levels and abilities, whether for recreation, exercise, relaxation or as an alternative part of a competition schedule. Of riders who ride once a week or less, 46 per cent cited access to safe off-road riding as a factor that would increase their riding opportunities.

It has to be acknowledged that riding is a sport with an element of risk, and potential risks increase when riding among other road and countryside users. However, riders at almost any level can hack out and enjoy the countryside from horseback as long as they are safe and in control under the supervision of an experienced Ride Leader.

Riding out can vary from a short hack along the lanes to many days in the saddle in the most extreme parts of the world. The British Horse Society (BHS), in association with NERN (the National Equestrian Route Network), works tirelessly to keep routes open across the UK for people to ride and in some cases even drive carriages on.

Riding on the road is often unavoidable; this means you will inevitably meet cars. Most drivers are considerate and will pass slowly, giving you a wide berth.

Benefits of hacking for horses

Hacking is brilliant for young horses as it introduces them to lots of new things and increases their understanding of the rider's aids. Once a horse has been backed and understands some basic aids, hacking out with an older sensible horse is a great way to improve his education. He will naturally want to follow the horse in front, which helps him to understand forward aids, and it will also teach him to respect the rider's controls by learning that it's fine to follow other horses, but not to the extent of 'chasing' them. It is also great way to desensitise horses of all ages. While out hacking, you may meet all sorts of things including cars, bikes, lorries, road signs, roadworks, farm machinery, wind farms, other animals and other 'scary' objects.

Not only does hacking introduce a horse to all kinds of objects, it can also be a great way to improve his way of going. While hacking it may be possible to incorporate hill work, which helps to develop strength, and riding on different and sometimes uneven surfaces, which helps with coordination and balance.

For a lazy horse, hacking out with others should encourage him to go forward so he can stay part of the herd. Many horses are often a little more active on a hack, which can be useful for practising bending or working on an improved outline if they lack motivation in the school.

While hacking, you may come across logs and other makeshift cross-country obstacles. These can be a great way to start to introduce the idea of cross-country jumping to a horse, as many youngsters are unlikely to have jumped previously in an open area. It can also provide the opportunity to test out a horse and rider's cross-country speed and rhythm and how well the horse jumps from it.

Hacking is also great for improving a horse's fitness. You can hack out for hours or minutes at whatever speed is appropriate to the horse's fitness. Many professional riders from the various disciplines hack out their top competition horses regularly.

Hacking provides variety in work and a chance to unwind for the competition horse.

Benefits of hacking for riders

General physical benefits of riding

Anyone who has ever taken up riding regularly will tell you that the most infuriating comment you can ever hear is 'but the horse does all the work …' This is obviously far from the truth: just as a car won't go anywhere without a driver, a horse will not move in a particular way unless told to do so, and on some horses and ponies that involves more work than others! A light trot metabolises enough rider calories to qualify as moderate intensity exercise.

A light trot metabolises enough rider calories to qualify as moderate-intensity exercise.

The physical benefits can be further categorised as follows:

Core strength. To stay balanced and keep from bouncing around in the saddle, the rider will have to use core muscles to maintain stability. This is an isometric exercise, which is where specific muscles are targeted to stay in a certain position.

Improved posture. As a result of sitting in these specific postures to keep balanced, it's likely that the rider's posture out of the saddle will improve the more regularly they ride.

Riding Out

Muscle tone. In addition to the core muscles, riding provides a good workout for the rider's back, inner thighs and pelvic muscles. This is mainly a consequence of the need to maintain a good position, coordinating with and controlling the horse's gait to help both rider and horse keep in balance.

Stable strength. Activities associated with riding such as mucking out, grooming, pushing wheelbarrows and carrying buckets also help to burn calories and improve strength.

Most yard duties involve physical exercise, helping burn calories and improve strength.

Mental benefits of riding out

For many riders, riding out in the countryside is an opportunity to relax and stop worrying about everything else in the world. This is reflected by the number of owners in the UK who

Hacking out is beneficial for both the rider and the horse.

own 'happy hackers'. It is also a great way for a rider to build relationships and trust in their horse and, more importantly, it is a lot of fun!

The psychological and social benefits of riding out can be further analysed along the following lines:

1. People are strongly motivated to take part in riding by the sense of well-being they gain from interacting with horses. This important positive psychological interaction with an animal occurs in very few sports.

2. Riding stimulates mainly positive psychological feelings. Both exercise and spending time with animals are activities believed to raise levels of the mood-enhancing hormone serotonin, so it's good for the body, brain and emotions.

3. Being outdoors and in contact with nature is an important motivation for the vast majority of riders.

4. There is existing evidence that additional health and well-being benefits can occur through forms of exercise, such as riding, that involve outdoor natural environments, contact with nature and interaction with animals.

5. A number of studies have found that the presence of natural settings can act as a motivating factor for physical exercise and possibly increase the intensity of exercise and the energy expended.

Enjoying the natural environment is good for the mind, body and emotional well-being.

Potential economic and business benefits

Horse-related sport and recreation is worth billions of pounds to the UK economy, and a recent survey shows that the uptake of riding holidays continues to rise. The numbers of British holidaymakers who stay local rather than going abroad has increased – a trend that looks set to continue. There is therefore a significant opportunity for landowners and farmers to benefit from this growing market by providing equine tourism opportunities on their land, and more and more opportunities for job openings in the equine tourism sector to become available.

Most riding schools offer a hacking option for riders who enjoy this form of exercise for relaxation and/or a pleasant way of enjoying the countryside. Many riders who enjoy hacking and riding out in the countryside are looking for a holiday where they can take their horse with them. Riding-related holidays incorporating bed and breakfast accommodation (for both horses and riders!), horse hotels and hunting holidays are popular options for both domestic and international visitors and the diversification of farms and livery yards into providing horse hotels is a growing industry.

The BHS runs a scheme called 'Horses Welcome' – the UK's first quality-assured scheme for equine bed and breakfast accommodation.

Above: *When a centre is approved by the BHS they will display an approved sign.*

Right: *Horse hotels enable riders to take their horses with them on holiday.*

Introduction

This initiative started in the south of Scotland in 2006 and has grown to include yards all over the UK and Ireland – all that demonstrate a commitment to providing a genuine 'home away from home' for horses. Anybody using a recommended yard can be confident that the premises have been inspected to ensure that the stabling, grazing and other facilities are of a suitable standard for visiting horses.

The scheme also provides access to central marketing, which complements the business's own promotional activities. Through regular newsletters, the BHS provides hints and tips from other members and offers networking opportunities to put members in touch with similar establishments in order to share ideas and knowledge.

The opportunities for employment in this sector of the equine industry and the need for qualified staff are greater than ever before.

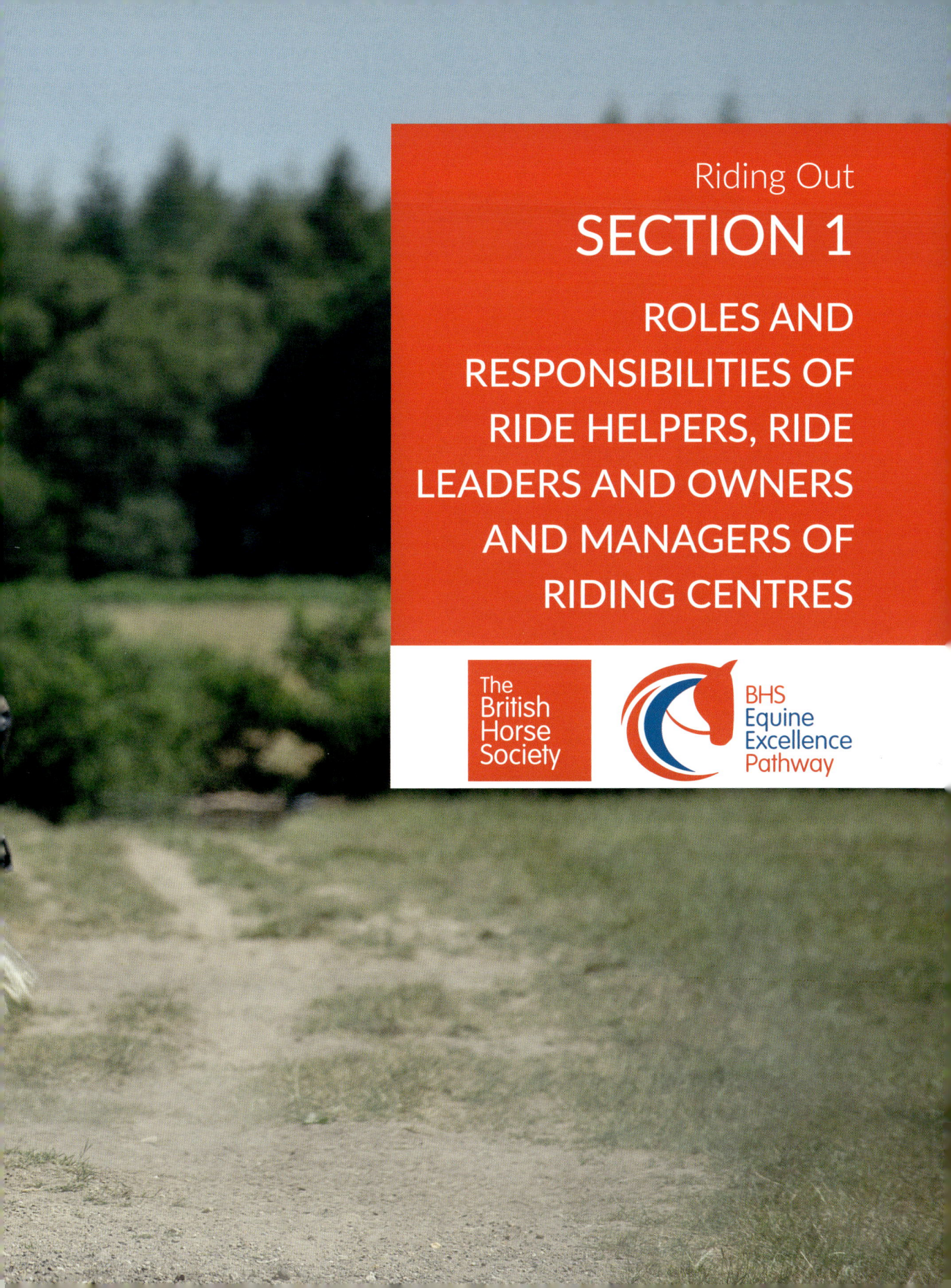

Chapter 1

Roles and Responsibilities of a Ride Helper

General duties

Staying safe around the yard

Summary

Roles and Responsiblities of a Ride Helper

As long as you have some equestrian experience, are happy to spend your day outdoors no matter what the weather, and are reasonably fit – then you should be able to consider the role of a Ride Helper.

Among the most crucial skills that you will need are willingness to be a good team member and to understand the importance of looking after the horses and ponies in your care to the best of your ability, as well as being pleasant and welcoming to the clients whom you meet in your daily work. You must be able to follow instructions carefully and completely in a timely manner and you will doubtless have to complete a number of sometimes repetitive tasks such as catching horses, grooming, tacking up and helping clients.

A good helper is one who communicates well and develops good relationships by listening carefully, and recording and passing on messages accurately and speedily. (The development of communication skills is dealt with in detail in the final chapter of this book.)

Above all else, you will need to be reliable and complete the jobs that you are asked to do, efficiently, always communicating any problems that occur at the earliest opportunity.

You need to be eager to learn and develop your skills, not being afraid to use your own initiative and yet willing to say when there is something you do not understand. It is important that you take a responsible attitude to safety, obey the safety code and stick to established good (safe) practices, never putting any other person or animal at risk.

As a Ride Helper there will be a number of different tasks for you.

General duties

On a daily basis, the kind of duties you may be asked to complete might include:

- Feeding and watering horses
- Mucking out
- Grooming
- Hoof care
- Rugging horses
- Saddling up
- Leading a horse
- Exercising horses
- Cleaning tack
- Keeping the workplace clean

Sweeping the yard as required throughout the day helps keep it tidy.

In addition to these daily tasks a Ride Helper may be asked to perform other tasks on a less regular basis, such as:

- Cleaning feeders and automatic waterers (buckets are cleaned twice daily).

- Washing walls and windows in stables to prevent dust build-up.

- Emptying and cleaning out feed room storage containers.

- Checking and cleaning gutters and drains.

Staying safe around the yard

Horse-handling can be dangerous if you don't consider a few basic facts. Always remember that the calmest horse or smallest pony has the potential to hurt someone if he is startled or scared. Above everything else you must take care to keep yourself and others safe while you are working on the yard.

If you always consider safety before you undertake even the smallest job, it will become a habit and may well prevent a nasty accident. As prey animals, horses' ability to react quickly and outrun predators was key to their survival in the wild. This instinct still remains strong in our domestic horses even though we make every effort to give them as safe an environment as possible to live in. They can become startled easily and remain upset long after whatever scared them has passed. Some horses are more reactive than others.

Rules for handling horses safely

- Be calm and quiet. Sudden movements or loud noises can cause a horse to jump or kick out.

- The safest way to lead a horse around the yard is with a headcollar and lead rope. It is important that you don't hook your fingers through any of the straps or rings, as if the horse pulls back, your fingers could be caught, injuring them or trapping your hand so you are dragged. Similarly, never wrap lead ropes, lunge lines, or reins around any part of your body.

- Never stand directly behind a horse. If you are brushing his tail, stand to one side and pull the tail gently towards you. When picking out feet or putting on leg bandages, don't kneel down on the floor as you will not be able to get out of the way if he moves suddenly. Bend over or squat down so that you can get out of the way quickly if necessary.

1 | Roles and Responsibilities of a Ride Helper

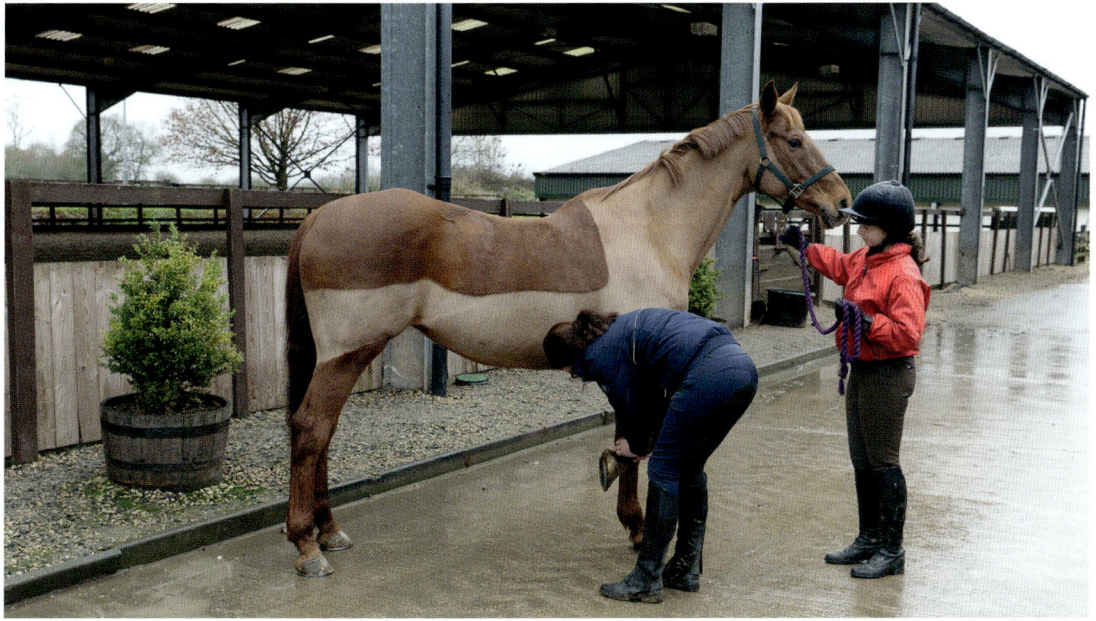

If you are holding a horse for someone, always stay on the same side as the other person and communicate with them.

- It is a good habit always to feed treats from a bucket. Horses can very quickly become greedy and mistake fingers for carrots.

- Wear sturdy shoes or boots that will protect your feet if a horse or pony steps on them. Never wear sandals or thin shoes around the yard!

- When grooming, tacking up, or mucking out, make sure you tie up the horse. When tying up a horse, always use a quick-release knot and tie him to a breakable loop – either string or a specially designed snap loop. That way if he gets scared and pulls back, he can quickly be freed. The feeling of being constrained can make a scared horse panic to the point of hurting himself or you.

- When you are leading a horse through a doorway, make sure the door is wide open and secured back so the horse doesn't bang his

Leading through a doorway; the door is opened wide and secured.

Riding Out

hips on it and it doesn't blow back onto him. This can startle the horse and result in you being trampled or dragged. If the door is narrow, go through first, make the horse wait, and then ask him to walk through after you as you stand to the side.

Leading a horse

When leading a horse with or without a rider it is important that care is taken to ensure your own safety, and the safety of those around you. The second bullet point on rules for safe handling apply here. Additionally, wear a hard hat, gloves and suitable footwear, and avoid wearing any clothing that might flap and startle the horse (e.g. a long scarf). If required carry a whip of appropriate length.

Horses can be led using a variety of different equipment or tack. When deciding what the horse should have on when being led, you need to consider the type of horse, where he is being led (for example, in an arena or on the road) and if the horse is being ridden.

In most circumstances when leading a horse, you should be on his left side, positioned near to the horse's shoulder. However, there are some situations when leading a horse on his right side is required. These may include when on the road, when leading two horses and, at times, when leading a rider.

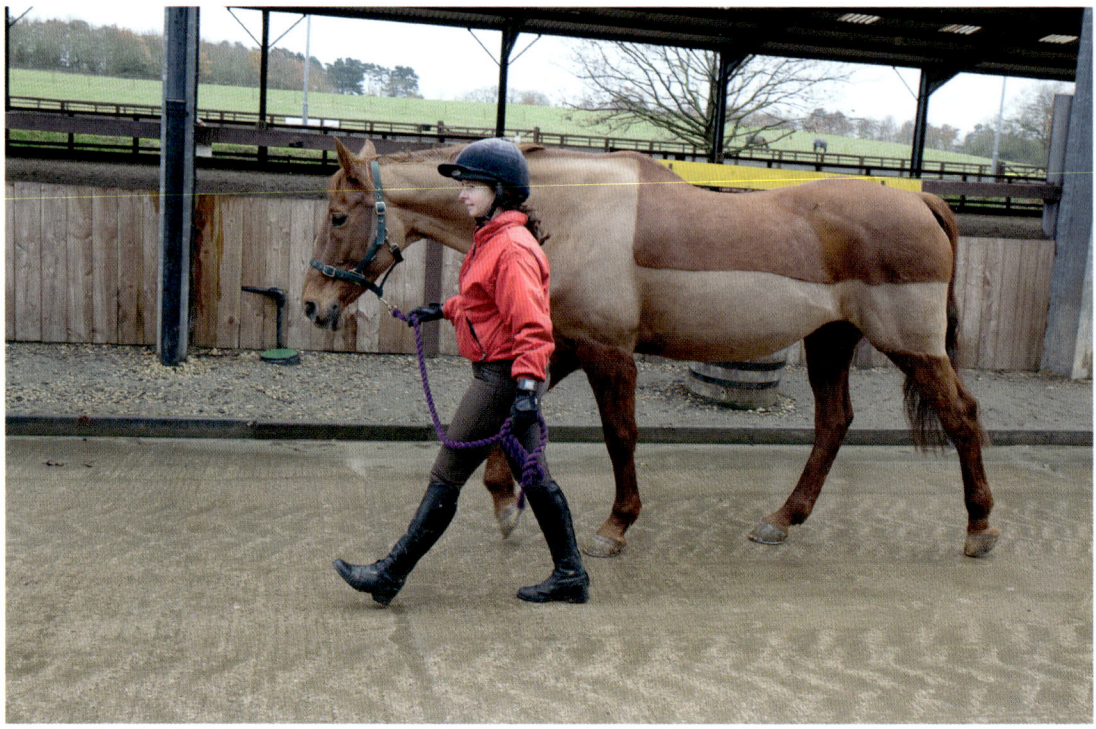

Leading a horse safely.

When leading a horse, the hand nearest to the horse's head (generally your right hand), should be positioned just behind the horse's jaw, holding the reins or lead rope securely as you walk next to the horse's shoulder. The loose end of the reins or lead rope should be held in the left hand, with the whip, if carried. Make sure the loose end of the reins or lead rope does not get so low that it could touch the ground or cause you to trip. However, the loose end should not be wrapped around your hand in case your hand gets trapped should the horse try to pull away.

Make sure you encourage the horse to walk beside you and that you do not get so close that you could get stepped on, or in front of the horse in any way. Look ahead in the direction that you are going and encourage the horse to move forward with your voice or, if required, a tap with the whip at the girth area.

When leading a horse with tack on, the reins should usually be taken over his head so that they can be held in both hands. However, if the horse is wearing a running martingale the reins should not be taken over the head. In this case, both reins should be held in one hand behind the horse's head.

Leading two horses

There may be times when it is necessary for one person to lead two horses together. This can be done safely so long as the horses are used to each other and calm together. When leading two horses in tack it may be safer to leave the reins over the horse's head as they would be when a horse is wearing a martingale. Hold the reins of each horse securely just under their heads, and stay between the horses level with their shoulders. Encourage the horses to walk at the same speed so that they walk side by side, but keep them a safe distance apart to maintain your own safety.

When leading a horse wearing a running martingale leave the reins on the horse's neck and use your right hand to hold both reins just behind the horse's chin.

When leading two horses, it is easier and safer to lead with the reins left over the horse's head as you would when a horse is wearing a running martingale.

Riding Out

Leading a rider

In general, when leading a rider on a horse the same basic procedures should be followed as when leading an unmounted horse. There are different types of equipment that can be used when leading a horse and rider; these may include attaching a lead rope to the horse's bit with a coupling or, in the case of a children's lead rein hack on ponies, fitting a headcollar, with lead rope, under the bridle with the noseband removed. When leading a rider you need to be able to keep control of the horse, and have a constant awareness of the rider and their security in the saddle, so regular looking back at the rider as well as being aware of where you're going is important. Although the rider may be receiving instruction from another person, you will still need to maintain communication with them and put them at their ease.

When leading a rider, make sure you regularly look back to check on the rider and communicate with them throughout the session to put them at ease.

When on the road, lead on the horse's right-hand side – this puts you between the horse and the traffic and provides you with more control to keep the horse over to the left-hand side.

The amount of control you need to maintain over the horse, and how much the rider has responsibility for control of the horse, will depend on the rider's ability, the horse's behaviour, and the environment. It will be different in an arena, in the open or on the road. When leading a rider it may be safer in some situations to lead on the right side of the horse. Reasons for this could be:

1. When on a public highway.

2. To stay on the inside when leading a rider on the right rein in an arena.

3. To be able to observe a rider on the right.

As your training progresses to the next level, you will also need to learn how to lead a rider when you, yourself are riding. How to do this is explained in the next chapter.

Summary

- Remember that, above everything else, you will need to demonstrate patience with both horses and people, develop good communication and observational skills, and it is an advantage for you to progress with your own riding ability.

- Always use safe, appropriate procedures and equipment that are suitable for you, the horse you are handling/leading and, where appropriate, the rider you are helping.

TRAINING TIPS

1. Try to find as many opportunities as possible to help out on different yards so you work with different types of horses and clients. If you are currently employed in one particular yard, opportunities to do this might arise when you are, yourself, on holiday.

2. Observe horses in different situations to learn how they react and behave; practise adapting the way you handle them depending on their behaviour.

3. When leading and handling horses in any circumstances, practise using safe procedures; try to remain by the horse's shoulder when leading, be positive and purposeful.

4. When possible, ask for feedback from experienced coaches who observe you leading and handling horses to help improve your technique.

5. Looking ahead to when you may graduate to becoming a Ride Leader, spend some time familiarising yourself with the surrounding area and with the equestrian sections of the *Highway* and *Countryside Codes*. (For further details on these topics, *see* Chapter 7.)

Chapter 2

Roles and Responsibilities of a Stage 2 Ride Leader

Yard duties

Leading rides

Summary

Riding Out

Roles and Responsibilities of a Stage 2 Ride Leader

The main role of a Stage 2 Ride Leader is to organise riding activities for groups of riders, and to escort those riders on hacks of up to about 2 hours. You may also have some supervisory responsibilities and might have to take temporary charge of the centre.

Hours are long and variable and can include evening and weekend work, although there is usually a seasonal element to hacking out.

The majority of the work will take place outdoors in all weathers, although some administrative duties will take place indoors.

While there is bound to be some overlap of stable work and leading rides, we will look first at the yard duties you may be expected to carry out.

Yard duties

It is important that you possess a common-sense approach to handling horses and are physically fit in order to ride for long periods and carry out yard work efficiently.

You should be capable of working under regular but not constant supervision and be able to care for stabled and grass-kept horses. The ability to do this will be supported by your knowledge of basic horse behaviour, including natural lifestyle in the wild, and the actions caused by his survival instincts in the stable, the school, the field and/or while out riding. Additionally, you will understand the value of regular inspections and what to look for first thing in the morning and last thing at night. You will know the signs of good and ill health in horses and ponies and recognise when they are off-colour or unwell, and comprehend the value of reporting such circumstances to a senior member of staff. You may also be asked to treat common horse ailments and/or assist a vet.

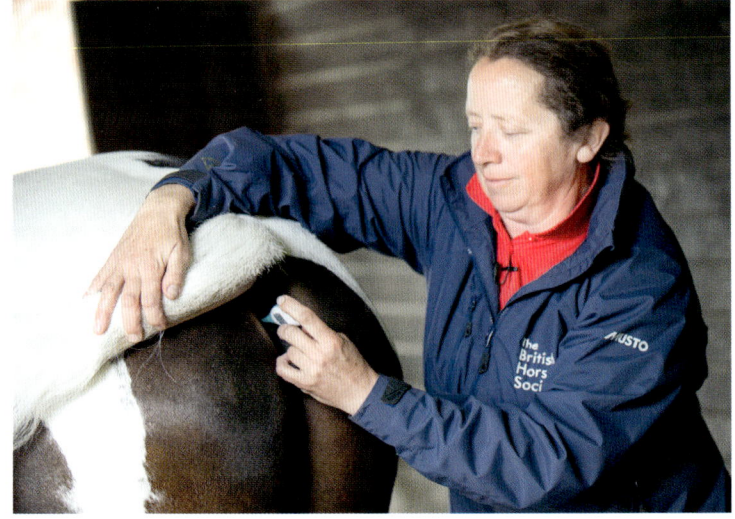

It is useful to keep a record of each horse's normal temperature, and you may be asked to take a horse's temperature if he is showing signs that he may be unwell.

2 | Roles and Responsibilities of a Stage 2 Ride Leader

You will be expected to assist in the daily running of a commercial yard, which may include helping with some of the administrative tasks, such as taking telephone bookings and dealing with minor accidents, queries and complaints. (Further details regarding bookings, accident procedures and communication skills are given later – *see* Chapters 3 and 11.)

You should be able to select and use relevant equipment that is fit for the purpose required and show that you can complete tasks in an industry acceptable, timely manner.

When working with clients and others you should always have the health, safety and welfare of people and horses as your top priority.

As you progress through this area of the industry, you will be expected to obtain qualifications in first aid and safeguarding (*see* Chapters 3, 4 and 11) in order to be employable in this field.

Your awareness of health and safety issues means that you will also have an understanding of fire precautions (*see* Chapter 3) and be able to describe the following correct procedure to adopt in the event of an accident.

Keep calm and assess the situation
Get help as soon as possible
Use common sense
Do not move the casualty, unless at risk
Keep loose horse(s) away from the casualty
Keep the casualty warm until help arrives
Support the casualty with comforting words
Check horse(s) over as relevant
Fill in an accident form once the casualty is handed on to first aider or medic
Understand what should be written on an accident form

Leading rides

As a Stage 2 Ride Leader, you may be expected to take out hacks of up to 2 hours on your own or to support a more experienced Ride Leader on longer hacks or treks that may take place over several days.

Hacking with a group of riders.

Key requirements and procedures for this role (additional to those qualities described above) can be summarised as follows:

- You should be able to organise a ride with a group of clients from the initial booking stage through to preparing for the ride out. As part of this process, you will assess the riders and then be able to supervise a small group of clients for a ride out (of no more than 2 hours duration). You should be able to pair suitable horses with riders based on size, temperament and ability. It is very important that you check the equipment of the horses and riders before you set out – you must have an up-to-date knowledge of the current hat standards and check that each rider is wearing suitable footwear as well as trousers that are not going to cause them discomfort. (Further details of these issues are given in Chapter 6.)

- During the ride, you must support any nervous or inexperienced riders as necessary and ensure the safety and welfare of clients and horses, which may include at a lunch stop (or, if you are acting as a support escort for a Stage 3 Trail Leader, even at an overnight stop).

Skills that will assist you to carry out these responsibilities include the following:

- It is useful for you to know how to read an Ordnance Survey map, use navigational aids such as GPS systems, and other tracking devices. You should be competent at planning a route and be able to consider eventualities if something goes wrong while you are out. These points are discussed further in Chapter 7.

- You should be able to plan the ride order of the horses and maintain this during the ride, while also being prepared to alter it if circumstances change and you need to support one rider more than others. You should make sure that all your riders are briefed on how to manage their distances between horses and that they have a fundamental understanding of basic procedures for crossing roads and dealing with hazards (e.g. other livestock, road users etc.) – *see also* Chapters 7 and 8.

- As stated earlier, it is very important that you are good at engaging with clients to create a positive, enjoyable experience for them so that they would like to repeat the exercise. However, there may be times when things do not go according to plan and you must have an awareness of how to deal with difficult clients, including outlining an appropriate complaints procedure.

- In order to fulfil your role, your own riding must be of a competent standard (for example, you should be able to ride with stirrups in walk, trot and canter in a balanced position independent of the reins, adopt a light seat in canter and jump a small fence) and you must be able to ride in an open space over a variety of terrain such as up and down hills as well as across fields, roads and bridleways. You must demonstrate that you are able to negotiate hazards/obstacles that you may come across, and open and close a gate.

Training for handling gates

The need for a Ride Leader to be adept at opening and closing gates is discussed in detail in Chapter 8, along with tips on how to deal with the different sorts that might be encountered. In general terms, the types of mounted movement required to deal with gates may already be part of your flatwork; if not your BHS Coach can help you with the turn on the forehand, leg-yield and rein-back. Opening gates can also be a functional way of teaching a horse these movements, so it is worthwhile practising them on any horse who might be used for leading a ride. The horse needs to be responsive to legs and hands, and many riders use their voice too, e.g. 'One step' when asking the horse to take one more step nearer the latch, or 'Stand' if it is necessary to use both hands for the gate.

Gate training is also an opportunity to improve your own balance and independent movements so that you can lean over without your legs moving or pushing into your horse, as that is likely to make him move away at the wrong moment. You can practise this off the horse, sitting on a wall or a substantial saddle horse, as well as on the horse – touching your toes, his tail and poll without moving your legs – with a helper to give you feedback and make sure you are safe should your actions cause the horse to move.

The following are some useful points to assist your training:

- If you do not have a gate available on which to practise, you can cover much of the requisite skill on any flat ground with a handy post, such as a jump stand, lamp-post or tree and a fence or wall that you can stand alongside. Having someone on the ground to help at first can be useful.

- Start by teaching the horse to stand still, with or without a hand on the reins. Having a horse who will stand for as long as you need is very helpful if you are fiddling with a latch. You can practise this at any time and place.

- Teach the horse to come close alongside a fence or other structure and stand at a given point. Teach yourself to bend low over your horse's shoulder, between him and the fence, without him moving away.

- Learn the turn on the forehand; then progress to turning one-handed while holding a post at normal hand height, then to turning while holding a post at gate height. Start with turning only one or two steps and progress to being able to turn a full circle with one hand low on the post.

- You also need to teach the horse to move sideways and backwards. You can practise backing alongside the fence as you move your hand along the rail, and moving sideways one-handed while leaning over, as if holding a gate.

Training to ride and lead

The skills of leading a horse and/or rider from the ground have been mentioned in the previous chapter. However, when taking a ride out, it may be necessary from time to time to lead another horse and rider from a mounted position, so all Ride Leaders should be competent at this exercise. Details of how to do this while on a ride, dealing with a group of riders in a practical situation and supporting and encouraging a rider who is experiencing problems, are discussed in Chapter 8 (and should be read in conjunction with this current note). However, it is clearly worthwhile practising the basic procedure at home before having to do so while out in the country, or on a road. It is also important to practise riding and leading with as many horses on the yard as possible, so that both you and the horses become accustomed to working in this manner.

As a Ride Leader you must learn to lead the other horse on the left-hand side of your own horse, and to constantly reassure the rider being led and explain everything before you do it in a calm manner.

When attaching the lead rope it is usual to dismount in order to manage both horses and to attach a lead rope (which needs to be long enough to accommodate the possibility of the led horse having to follow the leader's horse on a narrow track) through the offside bit ring to the nearside bit ring of the horse to be led, in order to have maximum control over both horses. After fitting the lead rope, you need to practise mounting while controlling both horses, and also leading a horse both alongside you and behind you – the latter in case you ever have to lead another horse on a narrow road or track.

When first practising, it is useful to have a senior member of staff or your BHS Coach on hand to give advice – if you have to do this on a ride, it needs to be done smoothly and efficiently.

It is important to practise riding and leading at home before having to do so whilst out on a ride. A senior member of staff or your coach can be on hand to provide advice.

Riding Out

Summary

- Ride Leaders are employed at over 3,000 riding schools or trekking centres all over the UK, especially in rural areas.

- Ride Leaders may be employed seasonally but could find work on a year-round basis if they have a coach's or instructor's qualification or if they are involved in the management or promotion of a centre during winter.

TRAINING TIPS

1. If you consider that this area of equestrianism is something you may be interested in, try to help in a yard that takes hacks out.

2. Offer to help prepare horses for riding out and act as a 'backstop' on a ride if your riding is of a sufficient standard.

3. Make sure that you read the parts of the *Highway Code* and *Countryside Code* that apply to riders. (*See* Chapter 7 for more details.)

4. Practise opening gates and leading another horse and rider while mounted.

Chapter 3

Roles and Responsibilities of a Stage 3 Trail Leader

General yard responsiblities

Key elements of health and safety procedures

Insurance

Summary

Roles and Responsiblities of a Stage 3 Trail Leader

As a Stage 3 Trail Leader, while you may be an employee at a large riding centre, it is also possible that you may be the manager of a yard or, indeed, a yard owner. With these possible variations of role in mind, please read the terms 'you', 'manager' and 'yard owner' in the following text as applicable to your circumstances. Please note, also, that while any Stage 3 Trail Leader should make themselves broadly familiar with the legislative requirements concerning health and safety related and insurance issues mentioned in the second part of this chapter, this becomes *imperative* for all managers and owners. Further to this, while this chapter provides a brief overview of key legislation, it is dealt with in greater detail in the next chapter.

General yard responsibilities

As a person with some authority on a yard, you should be able to look after a number of horses, clients and staff, under the remit of the equine industry's accepted protocols for working in the commercial environment. This should include the ability to take short-term charge of a centre in the manager's absence (if that is not your existing role). You should

Briefing the staff on the day's tasks.

understand how to care for stabled and grass-kept horses, train staff, work with clients and others while maintaining their health, safety and welfare on and off the premises. You will have to make sure that horses, stables, yards and fields are safe and in good order as well as organising the management of grassland and pasture for horses. The ramifications of fields, in particular, being unsafe/insecure are mentioned later in this chapter under public liability insurance.

You should be able to assess the tasks that the staff on a yard are completing and make sure that they are carried out in the most efficient, safe way. You should always be a good ambassador for the business, in terms of manner and appearance.

Liaising with clients and booking procedures

There are several ways in which a client may first make contact with a commercial yard, the most common being by means of a personal visit, or via telephone or email. At this stage, if they express an interest in what the yard has to offer, there needs to be a useful exchange of information between them and the yard's representative.

It is important to make a good first impression on new clients arriving at the yard, a welcoming smile and hello goes a long way.

Information for the client

Booking arrangements

To avoid misunderstanding by either party, it is important to explain your yard's charges and booking procedure. If you require new clients to undergo an assessment prior to their first ride out (*see* Chapter 6), you will need to explain this, and also explain how the time spent in the assessment relates to the time and cost of the ride out. For example, if a client is paying for a 2-hour hack, and the assessment (including horse allocation and associated preliminaries) takes half an hour, is that half-hour *in addition* to a 2-hour hack, or are they, in fact, getting a 1½-hour hack on this first occasion? If the latter, while most people are likely to be understanding of the desirability of the assessment, there is still potentially the issue of 'getting what one has paid for', and it is in everyone's interest to make such things clear beforehand.

Most commercial yards that book clients in to ride will require bookings in advance, sometimes with a deposit or full payment taken at the time of booking. Most yards will operate a strict 24-hour cancellation policy whereby, if a session is cancelled within 24 hours, the payment is non-refundable.

If a client has initially visited in person, it may be practical to take a booking there and then. Other than that, most yards will welcome bookings by either telephone or email. For many, email has become preferable as, on a busy yard without a dedicated secretary or receptionist, it is not always easy to answer the phone. Emails should be checked regularly – at least every morning, lunchtime and evening – and a response should be given as soon as practically possible, but always within 24 hours. For regular clients, it may be the case that a yard can offer group discounts or block booking reductions for a number of lessons. There are centres that also offer 'off peak' rates during times when the horses are usually quieter, such as midweek mornings.

Methods of payment

Most yards accept cash, cheques and card payments but also welcome BACs transfers from regular clients. More modern technology such as Apple Pay and other instant payments through mobile phones are becoming more popular. Yards may also take payment over the telephone. New clients may be asked to pay a deposit and, as mentioned above, there may be a system of charging a proportion or all of the fee for late cancellations – this is down to individual yard policy.

Required clothing

Particularly if the client is previously unknown to the yard, and dialogue reveals that they have limited previous experience of riding, it is important that the need for suitable clothing and equipment is made clear to them. Key requirements are:

- A correctly fitted riding hat to the current safety standard*. If the client does not have their own hat, many centres will hire or lend them one. It is advisable for staff at a centre that does this to attend a hat-fitting course.

- Appropriate footwear: riding boots or something with a slight heel (roughly 12mm/½ inch). Trainers are unsuitable for riding in.

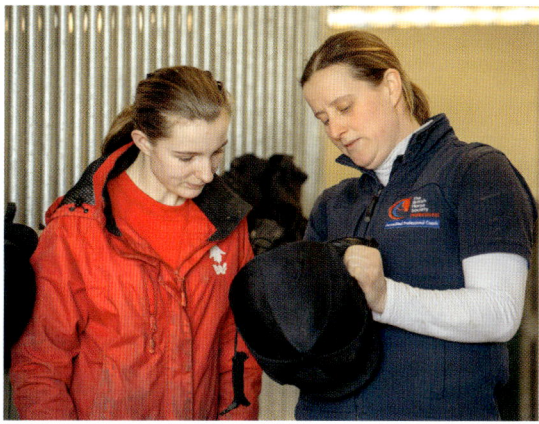 

Many yards have staff who have attended hat-fitting courses, so if a client wishes to hire a hat these can be fitted correctly.

Riding hat sizing			
Head measurement	Riding hat size	Head measurement	Riding hat size
49cm	6	57cm	7
50cm	$6^{1}/_{8}$	58cm	$7^{1}/_{8}$
51cm	$6^{1}/_{4}$	59cm	$7^{1}/_{4}$
52cm	$6^{3}/_{8}$	60cm	$7^{3}/_{8}$
53cm	$6^{1}/_{2}$	61cm	$7^{1}/_{2}$
54cm	$6^{5}/_{8}$	62cm	$7^{5}/_{8}$
55cm	$6^{3}/_{4}$	63cm	$7^{3}/_{4}$
56cm	$6^{7}/_{8}$		

> **Hat exemption**
>
> ** It is normal BHS policy to recommend that anyone riding a horse should wear a hard hat that complies with currently approved standards, and to insist that clients riding at BHS approved centres do so. However, Rule 49 of the **Highway Code**, which requires children under 14 to wear a hard hat while on the road, makes an exception to children under that age who are followers of the Sikh religion, and thus wear a turban. In the light of this, the BHS is prepared to make an exception for Sikh children wearing a turban, but they (or their guardian) must first sign a disclaimer absolving the riding centre of responsibility for any injury sustained as a direct consequence of this. It is recommended that this be kept on file.*

Good practice dictates clients wearing:

- Long-sleeved tops
- Gloves
- Back protectors. (In practice, it is not that likely that many 'casual' hackers/trekkers will have one of these, but their wearing should nevertheless be encouraged.)
- Jodhpurs/breeches are ideal, as they are designed for the purpose. Leggings may be a reasonable alternative, while fairly robust trousers, which are neither too tight nor too loose, may suffice in the short term.

And not wearing:

- Strappy tops
- Trainers
- Jeans or shorts
- Skirts of any description
- Hooded tops, which may interfere with rider's vision in windy conditions, and could be a danger if a rider falls near a horse's feet

Information for the yard

When a client first contacts the yard, it will be necessary for them to provide a few basic facts in order that you can advise them on the sort of riding likely to suit them, and to allocate them a suitable horse. You will need to know their approximate height and weight as well as their level of experience, and it can be useful if this is obtained in the form of a questionnaire, which can be kept on file. It also helps to take a contact number and email address for each client.

Establishing a client's previous experience as accurately as possible is very important. Many people who attend riding stables nowadays will have no prior experience with horses, and will be unaware of the limits of their own skill and competence. If someone is injured in a riding accident and someone else is to blame, they may be able to make a personal injury claim against the person at fault. The manager of the stable should take this into consideration and should not allow inexperienced riders to handle or ride wilful or hard-to-manage horses. If this were to happen and an incident occurred, then it is likely that the yard owner or manager could be accused of negligence and the client may be able to make a personal injury claim (*see also* Public Liability Insurance, later in this chapter). Such scenarios are clearly best avoided, so the owner/yard manager or responsible person on a stable yard should therefore take certain precautions to ensure that riders are not injured. These include:

- Ensuring that all horses offered out for riding have the appropriate experience, training and temperament. Where a horse has shown himself to be aggressive or has demonstrated a tendency to throw riders in the past, the yard owner should take account of this and should not continue to offer the horse out until the issue is addressed. Further to this, it is a requirement that any licensed riding centre (*see* Licenses, next chapter) must keep a list of horses approved for riding school/trekking use.

- Ensuring that all riders are provided with adequate safety equipment and are instructed on how to handle their horses.

- Ensuring that riders receive a health and safety briefing and are made aware of potential dangers and what they can do personally to reduce the risk of an accident occurring.

- Ensuring that there is a plan in place for dealing with accidents and providing first aid if someone is injured.

Failure to abide by these precautions could mean that the person responsible has acted negligently and, in the event of injury, this has opened them up to having a claim made against them.

Horse profiles

Most yards have a profile for each of their animals. These can be of assistance in matching horses to riders and, if they are included on the yard's website, they may enhance it and provide information for prospective clients. They can vary from a picture of each horse and a few lines of description on the website, to a much more in-depth document that identifies the kind of work the horse is used for, the breeding and the weight limit he can carry. It is important to keep these profiles updated, especially if the horse is receiving any kind of treatment or medication.

Key elements of health and safety procedures

Anyone who owns or operates a trekking centre, riding school, livery stable or any other kind of horse-related business needs to make sure that they are fully compliant with all relevant health and safety legislation. Failure to comply can result in the Health and Safety Executive undertaking a formal inspection or investigation and enforcement action can follow. The legal requirements of ensuring health and safety are examined in more detail in the next chapter (*see* The Health and Safety at Work Act 1974). However, in addition to the need for legal compliance, implementing sound health and safety measures can have wide-ranging benefits for a business, leading to increased profit and employee morale. The benefits of properly implementing health and safety rules include:

- Protection of workers on the yard.

- Saving absence costs and inconvenience caused by injury or illness.

- Saving recruitment costs.

- Protection of the reputation of the yard and the business.

- Improvements in productivity and overall business.

Health and safety considerations also mean that you should make the workplace as safe and comfortable as possible. This includes ensuring that the yard and any communal buildings are kept reasonably clean and hygienic, along with any toilets and kitchen facilities that may be provided. Attending to such details will be welcomed by staff and clients, and will add to your yard's reputation.

Principles of making the yard safe – risk assessments

Basically, the essence of health and safety regulations is that the business

Yard tools should have a designated storage space and should always be tidied away to prevent accidents.

should provide, so far as practical, a safe workplace for all employees. You must assess any risks the staff may encounter and take measures to minimise them. Where you are welcoming clients or other visitors to the yard, you should ensure that their safety is not put in jeopardy either.

Periodic risk assessments are one of the best ways to reduce risks in the workplace, and to ensure that the yard you are working on is fully compliant with health and safety obligations. The regular carrying out of risk assessments may also be a condition of a yard's employers' or public liability insurance (*see* later this chapter). While compliance is clearly important, the *fundamental aim* is to ensure that any risks are identified and measures for dealing with them are put in place.

The first step of an assessment is to identify any potential risks. Some of these will be obvious, but you should undertake a thorough examination of the stables, yard and any communal buildings and talk to employees in order to identify any less obvious hazards that could exist. You should also note down which groups of people are potentially at risk from these dangers.

Once you have identified any risks, you will need to determine what action you can take. You may already have safety measures in place, and if so you should assess whether or not these are sufficient; alternatively, the risk may not have been considered before, and you will have to decide what can be done to reduce or eliminate the hazard it poses. You may also want to ask staff what they think about proposed safety measures and if there are any unforeseen drawbacks.

You do not need to prepare for *every possible eventuality* or remove anything that could *conceivably be* a risk, but you must do what is reasonable – for example, on the basis of cost or the amount of time it would take – to reduce the likelihood of health and safety issues that might arise. You do not have to go to extreme measures to ensure safety if it is out of proportion to the actual risk. A simple example might be that you don't have to remove all hay forks from the premises, but you shouldn't leave them where someone might step on one. The law states you must do what is 'reasonably practicable', so if you feel that a safety precaution would be too expensive or take too long based on the actual likelihood of an accident or other safety issue arising, you probably do not have to act on it – or you could put a lesser measure in place. Note, however, as is emphasised in the next chapter, this does not mean you can avoid your responsibilities *simply by claiming that you cannot afford improvements*.

Once the risks have been evaluated, you can begin to implement solutions. If there are at least five employees, there is a legal requirement to document the details of a risk assessment in writing.

Risk assessments should be updated if something happens that could lead to new risks arising. For example, if new horses are brought into the yard, or a new cross-country course is built, there might be new hazards to be considered.

Riding Out

Risk assessment

ORGANISATION NAME

AREA/ACTIVITY (HAZARD)	PEOPLE AT RISK	CONTROL MEASURES IN PLACE	ACTION BY WHOM & WHEN

SUPPORTING YOU THROUGH EVERY STAGE

www.bhs.org.uk/pathways

Risk assessment examples

Who could be harmed?	Employee, client, visitor, contractor
What tasks are dangerous?	Jumping, galloping, lifting heavy articles
How often are those tasks carried out?	Daily, weekly or less frequently …
Does the task need to be done at all?	
If so, how could it be made safer?	Mechanical lifting of hay bales rather than manual lifting Use of a mechanical lift rather than a ladder

Answers to some of these questions can be found when looking at information/data on accident trends, for example the BHS accident map (http://www.bhs.org.uk/safety-and-accidents/horse-accidents/view-incident-map)

When assessing what control measures are in place or would need to be put in place, you should consider examples such as:

- Making sure staff are properly qualified.
- Implement manual handling training.
- Write down procedural controls, etc.

In general it is normally sufficient to comply with good or best industry practice such as those procedures laid out by the British Horse Society. However, it is also important to note that health and safety legislation is subject to change and, over time, requirements can be made stricter and practices and procedures that were once reasonably widespread may be judged unsafe. It will be your responsibility to be aware of these changes and to adapt procedures accordingly.

Fire prevention and procedures

Stable yards, by their very nature, can present a serious fire risk if they are not regularly checked and maintained. Hay, straw, electrical equipment and even cobwebs can all pose a fire hazard if appropriate fire safety measures are not taken.

Fire is every horse owner's worst fear; however the risk of fire can be dramatically reduced by following a few sensible precautions:

- Make sure the yard is a no-smoking area by erecting notices and reminding visitors.

- Develop a fire drill for the yard and test it out. This will allow you to work out solutions to potential problems – such as evacuating the horses – and ensure you have a clear procedure in place.

- Have electrical wiring and appliances tested and inspected on an annual basis and check to ensure that items like clippers and heaters are unplugged before leaving the yard.

- Remove cobwebs and dust on a regular basis – particularly from around the light fittings.

- Consider fitting fire and smoke alarms that can be easily heard – particularly if your yard is left unattended at night.

- If you are burning a muck heap or bonfire make sure you site it well away from the stables and damp it down completely before leaving it unattended.

- Check that you have the correct number and type of fire extinguishers located around the yard.

- Have your fire extinguishers tested or serviced on a regular basis so you can be sure they are in working order should a fire occur.

- If in doubt, arrange for your local fire safety officer to visit the yard and advise you.

- Have the procedure for dealing with a fire clearly displayed on the yard, including a contact phone number for the yard manager in the event of an emergency.

Check that the yard has the correct number and the different types of fire extinguishers required.

Accident procedures

Adherence to sound health and safety measures should minimise the risk of accidents or health risks, but total avoidance may not be possible, so measures must be in place to deal efficiently with any incident.

First aid

Suitable first aid provision is an important aspect relating to safety in the workplace. First aid is any medical attention given to someone at the scene of an accident, before emergency services arrive (if they are required). Part of the yard's risk assessment should involve deciding on how much medical equipment is required for your workplace and who is going to be nominated as a fully trained first aider.

> **A first aid box must, at minimum, contain:**
>
> - A leaflet giving general first aid guidance.
> - 20 assorted plasters.
> - 4 sterile triangular bandages.
> - A pair of disposable gloves.
> - 6 safety pins.
> - 6 medium-sized sterile dressings.
> - 2 large sterile dressings.
> - 2 sterile eye pads.
>
> The essential idea is that you must supply first aid provisions that are suited to the size, nature and any other considerations of your business.

Accident reporting

The Reporting of Injuries, Diseases and Dangerous Occurrences Regulations 1995 (RIDDOR), mentioned in more detail in the next chapter, impose a statutory duty on businesses to report certain types of injuries to the Health and Safety Executive. The list of injuries that are reportable includes; loss of consciousness caused by the ingestion of a harmful substance, electric shocks and chemical burns. However, the reportable injuries most likely to concern equestrian businesses are fractures, and the dislocation of hip or shoulder joints.

In addition to this, wherever there is an accident that results in a member of the public (which, in this context, includes members of staff) being taken to hospital, the Health and Safety Executive must be notified of this. It will also be necessary to complete an accident report form –see Accident and Investigation in the next chapter.

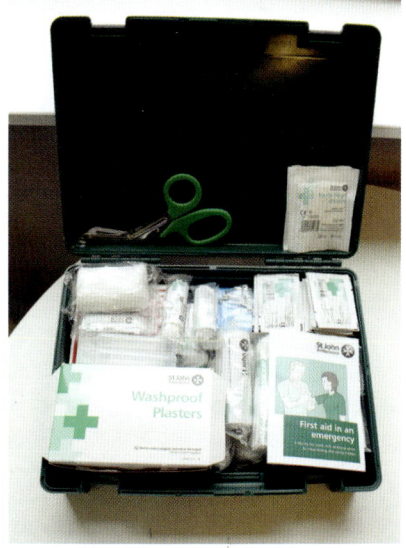

Supply first aid provisions suitable for the size and nature of your business.

Insurance

Maintaining correct levels of the appropriate insurance cover is of particular importance for the owners of horse-related businesses.

Employers' liability insurance

The Employers' Liability (Compulsory Insurance) Act 1969 requires all businesses that employ people in any capacity to hold employers' liability insurance. The minimum level of cover that a business must have in order to trade legally is £5 million and, in many cases, businesses will have at least £10 million in employers' liability cover. This insurance was implemented to guard against businesses acting recklessly with regard to the health and safety of employees, and then being unable to meet compensation claims when employees were injured.

Public liability insurance

Under what are now Defra regulations (formerly the Riding School Act) all riding centres have to be registered and one requirement of this is that they must have public liability insurance. Every horse owner is liable for any damage caused by a horse they own where that damage results from negligence. This might be the case where a horse owner keeps aggressive horses in a field through which a public right of way runs, or fails to provide adequate warnings about horses who are known to be dangerous (for instance, liable to bite). A horse owner can also be liable for nuisance if horses are allowed to escape onto a neighbour's property.

Unfortunately, accidents do happen, and if an accident occurs, the business could face a potentially expensive claim. Public liability insurance will protect the yard owner against any claims made by a member of the public or client if they have suffered a loss or injury as a result of an incident under the yard's remit. Not only will the insurance cover the cost of any compensation awarded to the claimant, it will also cover costs, fees and expenses involved in the claim – taking away the hassle and worry of what ordinarily would be a very stressful time with potentially ruinous consequences.

It is important to note that public liability insurance may not cover claims made specifically in the context of negligence. Even legal professionals admit that negligence can be a complex issue, and it can be a claim that has to be considered on a case-by-case basis. Sensible practice would be to ensure, so far as possible, that no claim in negligence can be made against you, and to bear in mind that, were one to proceed, you should be certain that your insurance would cover it.

3 | Roles and Responsibilities of a Stage 3 Trail Leader

Recommending insurance to clients

Many riders, especially relative newcomers, are not aware of insurance issues in connection with riding. Even if they are riding horses on hire from a riding centre, and accompanied by a representative from that centre, there could conceivably be instances where some action or omission of their own gave rise to a claim against them personally. Because of this, it may be prudent to draw clients' attention to the desirability of taking out their own personal liability insurance.

Such insurance is one of the many benefits of joining the BHS.

Summary

- The skills needed for a Ride Leader – even those taking out relatively short hacks – are primarily those surrounding safety and efficiency for riders and horses in your care. You need to develop a rapport with people, especially those you have not met before.

Riding Out

Riding out can be a great opportunity to make new friends.

TRAINING TIPS

1. Try to talk to as many new people as possible so that you become confident with strangers as well as your friends and colleagues.

2. Practise 'role playing' with given scenarios so that you can deal with different situations as they arise.

3. Work with the other members of staff on a yard to become more efficient and improve your time management together.

4. Engage in self-reflection – explained in more detail in Chapter 11.

Chapter 4

Legislation

The Health and Safety at Work Act 1974

Fire safety

Accident reporting and investigation

Safeguarding

General Data Protection Regulation (GPDR)

Licences

Summary

Legislation

In this chapter we will look further at legislation applicable to riding centres, expanding on some themes which were touched upon in the previous chapter.

The Health and Safety at Work Act 1974

Within the UK there is a legal framework to support the process of managing the safety risks that individuals are exposed to, and riding centres are no exception. The Health and Safety at Work Act 1974 (HASAWA) states that employers must protect the 'health, safety and welfare' of all on their premises, including temporary staff, casual workers, the self-employed, clients, visitors and the general public. However, these duties are qualified with the words 'so far as is reasonably practicable'. It is worth noting at this stage that many riding establishments/livery/hacking or trekking yards operate on low margins and, in economic terms, the cost of implementing health and safety controls must be proportionate to the risks. However, there is a balance to be struck here because, while the wording of the Act may mean it is possible that employers can argue that the costs of a particular safety measure are not justified by the reduction in risk that the measure would produce, it does not mean that they can avoid their responsibilities simply by claiming that they cannot afford improvements. Further to this, you should note that many health and safety requirements carry 'strict liability', meaning that there is no valid defence for failing to meet them. In addition, a failure to comply fully will weigh heavily against you in any civil claim for compensation if someone is injured while on your premises, or one where you have any authority to work.

The basic requirements are for establishments to have systems in place to manage any risks that are likely to occur, to consider ways to lessen the likelihood of these happening and to make sure everyone is aware that these controls are in place. This means that all yards must:

- Have a written health and safety policy (if employing five or more people), that also includes any volunteers.

- Make assessments of the risks to employees, clients, contractors and any other people who could be affected by the activities of the yard – and record the significant findings in writing (if employing five or more people).

A risk assessment must be 'suitable and sufficient', i.e. it should show that:

- A proper check was made.

- Anyone who might be affected was consulted.

- All the obvious significant hazards were dealt with, taking into account the number of people who could be involved.

- The precautions are reasonable, and the remaining risk is low.

If your risk assessment identifies a number of hazards, you need to put them in order of importance and address the most serious risks first, and identify long-term solutions for the risks with the biggest consequences, as well as those risks most likely to cause accidents or ill health. You should also establish whether there are improvements that can be implemented quickly, even temporarily, until more reliable controls can be put in place. It is important that you regularly review your risk assessment and make sure it stays up to date, as few workplaces stay the same. Sooner or later, you may bring in new horses, find new routes to take rides on, or change staff, and such issues could lead to new hazards.

Factors to consider when complying with the legislation

Here, we look at key meanings of terms used in the The Health and Safety at Work Act 1974.

Staff

In respect of this legislation, 'staff' include full- and part-time paid employees and those undertaking voluntary work. Furthermore, in terms of applying health and safety legislation, a verbal contract rather than a written one is sufficient to demonstrate an employer/employee relationship. Generally, employees who are a members of the same family as the employer are covered by the legislative requirements. Staff roles vary considerably, from assistance with handling or riding horses, mucking out stables, grooming, preparing for lessons, to instructing and administration. Many of the assistants and volunteers will be teenagers, parents and children.

It is a legal requirement under the Management Regulations of the Act that specific, rather than generic risk assessments are undertaken for young people (defined as under the age of 18) and children (below minimum school leaving age) to reflect their vulnerability and inexperience with regard to risk http://www.hse.gov.uk/youngpeople/law/). These assessments should be discussed with their parents/guardians. *See also* Safeguarding, below.

It is worth noting that a minority of establishments have sought ways around health and safety and other obligations towards volunteers, by describing them as club members, etc. An evaluation of the exact circumstances will be necessary when consideration of the need for a riding school/centre licence is under discussion. *See also* Licences, later this chapter.

Contractors

Those who are likely to visit a yard on a frequent basis include vets, farriers, suppliers of feed and bedding, maintenance contractors and field contractors (to cut hay, top fields, maintain hedges and ditches). While some would have knowledge and awareness of the relevant risks, there are still steps that proprietors can take to control these risks.

Clients/riders

In terms of riding centres, it is likely that the clients will be either riders or potential riders. These usually fall into one of the following categories:

- *Beginners* – those new to riding or who have ridden for just a short period.

- *Novices* – those with more riding ability than beginners but still lacking in experience.

- *Experienced* – those with reasonable ability and experience, usually familiar with areas such as showjumping and cross-country jumping. It should be noted that sometimes experienced riders will have had an absence from riding and may need a period of refreshing.

In addition to considering individuals' actual riding experience, account should be taken of aspects such as age, and the existence of any disability.

Of course, the act of riding itself can present significant hazards. Riding can range from simply walking or trotting within a purpose-built area, to galloping at speed or trotting along roads in close proximity to moving vehicles. Novices, for example, have much to learn and may not have established balance when riding, so could be more easily unseated than a more experienced rider.

Higher risk	Lower risk
Inexperienced rider	Experienced rider
Working at speed e.g. galloping or cantering	Walk and trot
Open field or areas such as beaches and moorland	Indoors school/enclosed outside areas
Jumping fences, both showjumping and cross-country	Working on the flat
Inexperienced horse or temperamental type of horse	Older experienced horse
Road traffic	Non-traffic environment

4 | Legislation

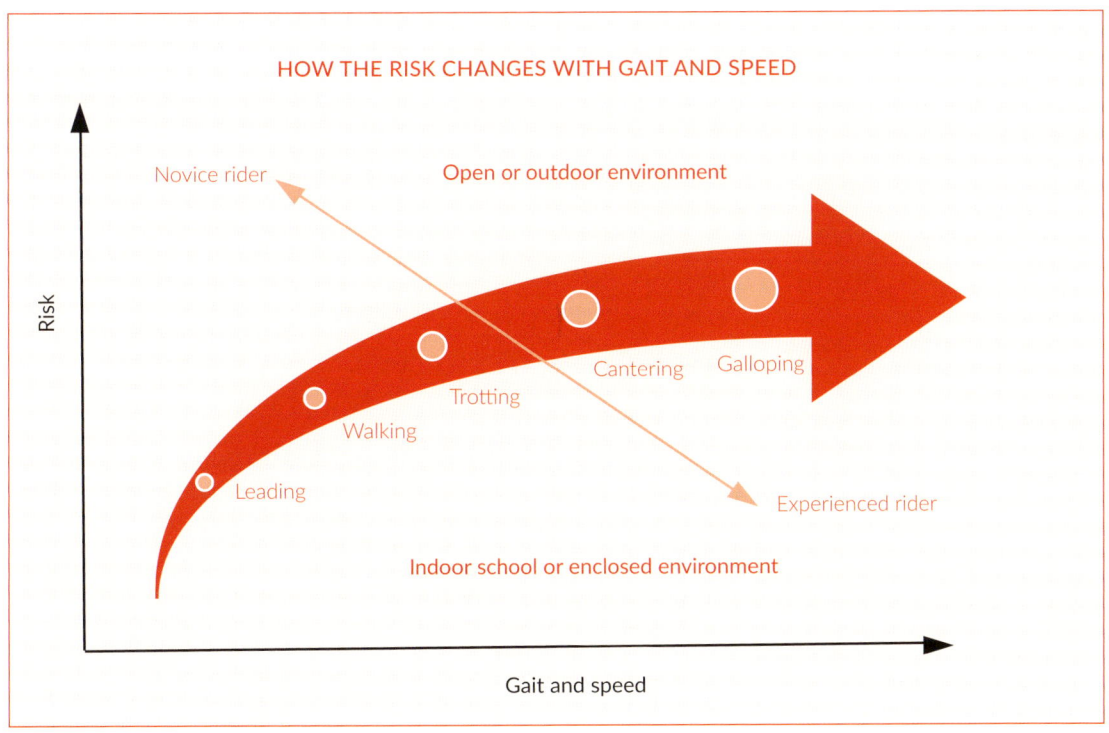

Members of the public

This definition may include friends or relatives of people keeping their horses at livery, children and young persons and other people visiting the yard/watching events, etc. There is likely to be a vast array of experience among these people, ranging from competent riders to those completely unfamiliar with horses and the associated risks. Again, they will be representative of all sectors of the community and may, for example, include people with disabilities. Children and people unaccustomed to horses may need particular protection because of their lack of understanding/experience of the hazards associated with horses.

Hazards

These are 'something that has the potential to cause harm or injury'. Of course, any horse has the potential to cause harm or injury, whether deliberately or not, and since horses can have different temperaments this means that they react to different stimuli and can be quite volatile. It is generally considered that breeding can affect the manner in which a horse behaves, and as a generalisation, Thoroughbred types can be flighty and strong-willed and cobs more hardy and calm. Hopefully, it will be calmer types who make up a considerable proportion of the animals used for riding out. However, horses are ultimately herd animals with a flight instinct, so an element of unpredictability can never be ruled out. The environment in which riding typically takes place can include uneven/cobbled floors, barbed wire fences, dark mornings/evenings as well as inclement weather, each of which presents its own hazards. In addition, the typical operations that are carried out in any establishment present hazards. These can include loading and unloading into horseboxes, catching horses from the field, moving parts of equipment and the use of machinery.

Fire safety

The Regulatory Reform (Fire Safety) Order 2005, which came into effect in 2006, applies to England and Wales and there is equivalent legislation covering the remainder of the United Kingdom. The occupiers of all equestrian establishments, regardless of whether they require a licence to operate, must ensure a competent person undertakes a suitable and sufficient fire risk assessment. Again, where there are five or more employees the findings of the risk assessment must be recorded and acted upon.

Lightning strikes and arson-set fires contribute to several thousand fires per year to the UK's equestrian and agricultural premises. The people at risk again include staff, visitors and contractors, and people not authorised to be on the premises.

Specific hazards will usually include potential ignition sources such as hot shoeing by farriers, electrical and mains gas installations and appliances, smoking, heating and lighting sources, cooking, live flames, vehicles and their exhausts, LPG gas in cylinders, some veterinary supplies, firearms and ammunition. Combustible hazardous materials include quantities of fodder and bedding (e.g. hay and straw, wood-based bedding), storage of LPG cylinders and other gases, chemicals, vehicle fuel oils and petrol, vehicles parked against buildings and flammable decorating materials.

The risk to life from fire is an important element of the fire risk assessment and will include daytime occupancy fire risks to staff and visitors, residential accommodation for visitors and clients, overnight accommodation (which will include riding B & B and horse hotels), seating accommodation within riding schools and restaurants, special arrangements for Riding for the Disabled groups, etc. Fire safety standards for residential accommodation would normally mirror those of a hotel.

Accident reporting and investigation

Any incident on the yard or while out riding should be recorded and documented for possible future investigation and also to inform managers of situations that may need attention. In the worst case scenario the accident could result in a claim being made, so it is important to obtain and list the names, addresses and telephone numbers of any witness(es), including other people on the ride. Most organisations will have a specific form to be completed that will record the following types of information:

ACCIDENT FORM

Person involved: Name: _____ Age: _____

Address: _____

_____

Name of establishment/location: _____

Reference number: _____ Date of accident: _____ Time of accident: _____

Full name of proprietor/owner of premises: _____

Full name of instructor/escort: _____ Qualification(s): _____

Name of horse/pony: _____ Sex: _____ Age: _____ Height: _____

Owner of horse/pony: _____

Instructor's/escort's report: _____

_____

_____

How accident happened: _____

_____

_____

A sketch plan showing position of other horses, people, equipment, gates, etc. is helpful.

How long had the lesson/ride been in progress? _____

Comments of person involved immediately after incident: _____

_____

Did the person remount and complete the lesson/ride?   YES ☐   NO ☐

If not, what action was taken? _____

_____

Was medical assistance   Offered ☐   Accepted ☐   Refused? ☐

Was hospital or doctor involved?   YES ☐   NO ☐   (If YES – which)? _____

Instructor's/Escort's signature _____ Date: _____

Signature of person completing the form: _____

Print name: _____

Position held: _____ Date: _____ Time form completed: _____

Subsequent developments including medical reports, if known: _____

_____

RIDDOR

Under the Reporting of Injuries, Diseases and Dangerous Occurrences Regulations 2013 (RIDDOR), certain specified injuries/events have to be reported to the relevant enforcing authority:

- Fractures, other than to fingers, thumbs and toes.

- Amputations.

- Any injury likely to lead to permanent loss of sight or reduction in sight.

- Serious burns (including scalding), which cover more than 10 per cent of the body or cause significant damage to the eyes, respiratory system or other vital organs.

- Any scalping requiring hospital treatment.

- Any loss of consciousness caused by head injury or asphyxia.

- Any other injury arising from working in an enclosed space which leads to hypothermia or heat-induced illness or requires resuscitation or admittance to hospital for more than 24 hours.

Safeguarding

It is important that we make sure that people working with children and vulnerable adults are suitable people to do so. The BHS's aim is to ensure that everyone can enjoy horses in a safe environment, protected from harm, and there are measures in place to avoid unsuitable people being able to gain access to young people.

Throughout the UK and Republic of Ireland criminal record checks are a requirement for staff and volunteers who are supervising or teaching young people under the age of 18.

All staff who are left in charge of young people under the age of 18 in England and Wales should have had a DBS check. Previously known as a Criminal Record Check, the Disclosure & Barring Service will check to see if the person has any criminal and/or police records and any relevant information about criminal convictions and cautions will be included on the DBS report.

General Data Protection Regulation (GPDR)

This legislation was introduced to standardise and strengthen data protection policies for residents of EU member nations. Although it's not possible to be certain of the UK's future status at the time of writing, it seems likely to remain in place in the future. The term 'data' refers to any personal information stored by any business. This includes that of staff, volunteers, suppliers, clients and anyone else involved in the business. If a yard has employees, then the owner/manager will hold their contact and bank details – that's data. Staff performance reviews, attendance records, volunteer names and addresses, lists of people the business has helped or want to contact – it's all data and it all counts!

Ignoring the requirements of GDPR legislation risks a fine of up to £20 million or 4% of annual turnover – whichever is the greater. GDPR applies to all organisations. There is a misconception that if organisations are small, or volunteer-based or only have paper records, they are exempt. This is not true. No data controller or data processor is exempt.

Licences

Any riding establishment that hires out horses or ponies for riding, trekking or a riding school needs to have a licence from their local authority, which needs to be renewed every year. The fee and specific conditions are set by local councils, but there are some common rules and requirements. The person who holds the licence must possess an appropriate formal qualification, or have sufficient demonstrable experience, in the management of horses, as well as holding a valid certificate of public liability insurance (*see* Chapter 3), which must also be displayed. (The running of the business must never be left in the charge of anyone who is under 18 years old and no horses should be hired out except under the supervision of a person aged 16 years or more, unless the licence holder is satisfied that the person hiring the horse is competent to ride without supervision.)

The horses used at the establishment must be:

- In good health and physically fit.
- Suitable to be hired out and used for riding.
- Provided with adequate food, drink and bedding.
- Regularly exercised.
- Safeguarded in an emergency.

There needs to be evidence of liability insurance that covers any injuries, and a register of all horses on the premises (including those aged 3 years or under, who cannot be used for riding at that age).

There are also certain stipulations regarding the welfare of the horses, and it is an offence to:

- Hire out a horse, or to use a horse for the purpose of providing riding lessons in return for payment or for demonstration riding, if the horse is in such a condition that being ridden is likely to cause the horse suffering, or if the horse is less than 3 years old, is a mare in foal, or has foaled within the preceding 3 months.

- Fail to provide suitable care for sick and/or injured horses kept for the purpose of hiring out, for the purpose of providing riding lessons in return for payment or for demonstration riding.

- Supply defective equipment, for a horse who is hired out, and which is likely to cause suffering to the horse.

BHS approved status for centres offering riding out/hacking

Further details on this issue can be found on the BHS website bhs.org.uk, and are updated regularly in line with current legislation. Key points for information are:

1. All riders to wear a correctly fitted riding hat to the current standard and footwear designed for riding that is deemed safe. (*See* the exemption for children of the Sikh religion wearing turbans, subject to a disclaimer, mentioned in Required Clothing in Chapter 3 and *Highway Code* Chapter 7.)

2. All centres have to have documentary evidence that all riding out activities and routes are risk-assessed and this information is provided to ride escorts/leaders in advance.

3. All escort staff must hold the British Horse Society Ride Safe Certificate.

4. All escort staff must be first aid qualified, must carry a portable ride leader first aid kit and a mobile phone for use in emergencies.

5. The use of high visibility equipment is mandatory for horses and riders when riding out (*see* panel across).

6. Staff must possess BHS Stage 2, BHS Ride Leader Level 2, Pony Club B Test or have appropriate professional experience.

7. Centres must undertake centre-specific training (supported by a training log book) and

assessment by a BHS Stage 3 Coach in Complete Horsemanship (previously known as BHSAI) of the Ride Leader/Escort's competence. The training and assessment must include, as a minimum, ride supervision, riding ability, age and incident management, such as riding and leading.

There are further criteria relevant to centres offering 'treks'. A trek is defined as a ride of longer than 2 hours duration, covering more than 16 km (10 miles) or starting remotely from the yard location, and may be more adventurous in nature e.g. pub rides, beach rides. The criteria are:

1. BHS Stage 3 Coach or BHS Ride Leader Level 2 or 3 are the minimum qualifications for someone leading such rides.

2. For Escorts/Ride Leaders who do not hold BHS qualifications, during the first six months of employment, a centre must undertake centre-specific training (supported by a training log book) and assessment by an Equestrian Tourism Centre Manager (ETCM) of Ride Leader/Escort competence or BHS Stage 3 Coach in Complete Horsemanship. The training and assessment must include, as a minimum, ride supervision, riding ability, age and incident management. In such situations, a formal BHS qualification must be obtained during the following 6 months.

> *** High visibility clothing**
>
> *High visibility clothing really is some of a rider's most important equipment, and should be worn out hacking at all times. It enables drivers, cyclists and walkers to see riders significantly earlier, which gives them time to slow down and pass carefully and safely. High visibility kit can be a major safety factor not only on the roads. If, for example, a rider has a fall while cantering across open moorland and is injured or unconscious, or if a mist descends suddenly in hill country and the rider becomes lost, high visibility clothing will make it easier for people searching for them.*
>
> *Nowadays electronic tags are available that attach to the saddle and connect to the mobile phone of nominated contacts. If the rider falls off, the contact is interrupted and the contacts are notified with a grid reference.*
>
> *There are many different kinds of high visibility kit available for horse and rider, and a selection of colours. It is important to know the difference between fluorescent and reflective clothing. Fluorescent materials show up in the daylight but have no special qualities in the dark, whereas reflective materials will reflect a light source in either the day or night, so are essential during fading daylight hours and at night. Rules 50 and 51 of the* **Highway Code** *give more information about what to wear on the road –* **see** *Chapter 7.*

Riding Out

Summary

- The BHS has a special category within its approval system for centres that offer hacking. By becoming BHS approved, there is a guarantee that your premises and staff have all met with our strict standards of safety, horse welfare and tuition.

- All BHS Approved Centres are regularly inspected to ensure they meet high standards of safety, horse welfare and tuition.

- For added peace of mind, it also means that every centre is insured for public liability and complies with the latest health and safety legislation.

- This way we can be sure that everyone will be inspired to enjoy the best equestrian experience.

TRAINING TIPS

1. Make sure you are confident in the procedures involved in the event of any accidents or incidents.

2. Practise filling out some of the forms and ask an experienced person to check that you have completed them correctly.

3. Go on the relevant websites to keep up to date with any changes in the legislation as it applies to you in your working role.

4. Try to get into the habit of logging any long rides of over 2 hours or those that have particular issues to deal with – such as loose horses out in a field, roadworks, etc.

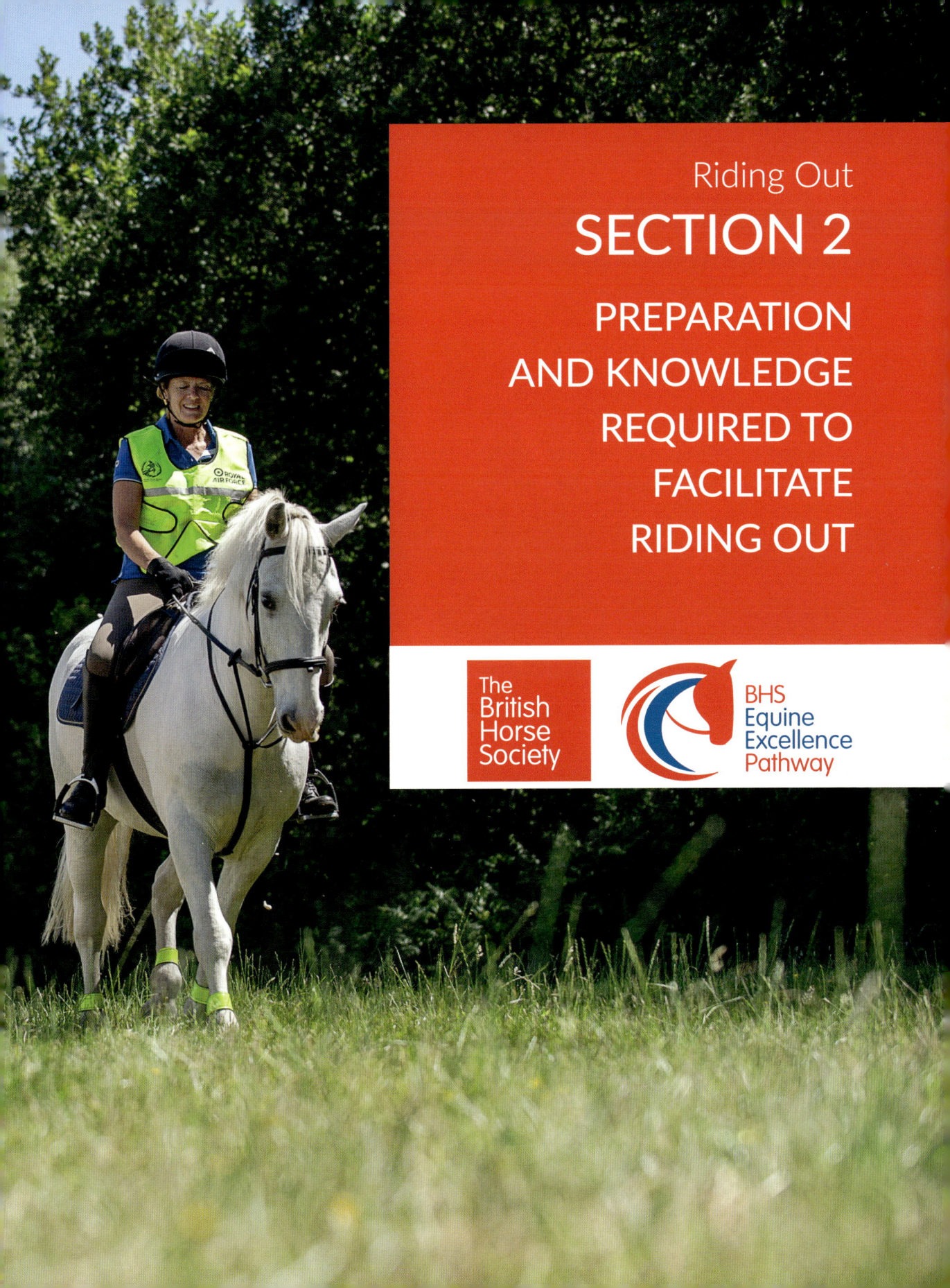

Chapter 5

Training and Fittening Horses for Riding Out

Manners

Fittening

Summary

Riding Out

Training and Fittening Horses for Riding Out

As with all equestrian disciplines, the horse and ponies used for hacking or trekking need to be sufficiently well schooled and fit enough to do the job well, both for their benefit, that of their riders and, indeed that of the centre's owner, since healthy, well-mannered horses will enhance the centre's reputation and help to keep veterinary bills to a minimum. While they do not need to be dressage champions or to jump big showjumps, it is crucial that the fundamental basics are established.

Manners

It is very important that horses used by commercial centres for taking out clients have good manners. While it is true that any horse can be unpredictable, we need to have those who will be as reliable as possible. When on a remote bridleway or hillside, the horses must be trustworthy and behave in a consistent way through most situations. This reliability must extend to anything the horses are likely to encounter in their locality. Passing various livestock, for example, is dealt with in Chapter 8 but there are other scenarios to which they might have to become accustomed, such as passing wind farms and crossing high bridges over busy motorways.

Further to the question of manners, horses must, of course respond readily to the aids for all basic movements.

Standing still

A horse used for hacking out should stand still when asked to do so, especially while riders mount or wait to cross a road. One of the joys of hacking out is to be able to stop and admire the scenery, or chat to people along the way. Therefore, horses must be taught to stand quietly. In teaching this to an individual horse, you should use every opportunity to ask him to stop what he is doing and wait until *you* ask *him* to move on (i.e. the decision is yours, not his). A verbal command is useful to reinforce this training and you need to differentiate between 'Whoa', which asks for him to stop moving and 'Stand' for when he is immobile. During the initial training, you could use an immovable object such as a wall, fence or tree to walk towards and ask the horse to halt and stand in front of it.

Leading

As a Ride Leader, there will be many times when you are out and about when you may need to dismount and lead your horse – and there could be occasions when it is necessary for those you escort to dismount and lead also. Therefore, all horses should so be happy to be led (from both sides) without stepping on the person leading, pulling back, or marching off faster than the person leading them can walk. Further to this, they should learn to walk happily at the speed of the person leading, no matter how fast or slow that is, as the terrain they may be walking on might vary enormously.

This, again, is something worth practising at home with individual horses. If, at first, a horse tends to pull back or lags behind you, you may need to carry a long schooling whip so that you can 'flick' him with it to encourage him to keep up. If he walks too fast, short, intermittent pulls on the reins should prevent him from pulling against you, so that you can allow the rein to slacken when he is walking at your speed.

Since, when riding out, there may be situations when horses have to be dismounted and led past a frightening obstacle, a good grounding is important – especially when riders having to do this may be quite inexperienced at such things. You could practise with obstacles in the arena, tarpaulins on the ground, etc., to give horses some familiarity with the idea. An important aspect of this training is that the person doing the leading should look ahead rather than at the obstacle itself, and this should be explained to riders if such a situation arises on an actual ride out.

When leading past an obstacle, look ahead and not at the obstacle itself; the horse will then be less likely to react.

Picking up feet

It is important that horses will pick all four feet up without a fuss as you may have to remove stones or compacted mud or ice from their feet while you are out, or even remove a shoe in an emergency, or fit a hoof boot. If the horse's legs are always tapped before their feet are picked up, they will learn to lift the appropriate foot without you having to run your hand right down leg – this may be a real bonus when you are out and legs are muddy!

Moving sideways and backwards

If the horses will move backwards or sideways when asked to do so, this will make life much easier when you are riding out. You, or other riders as necessary, will for example, be able to position a horse against a log to remount from, and it will be easier to negotiate gates, whether mounted or on foot. Initially, it helps to train horses from the ground, getting them used to moving over in the stable by applying pressure to one side with your hand and using the command 'Over'. Once they understand the basic principle, you can refine this from the saddle by introducing turns on the forehand or haunches and some elementary leg-yielding.

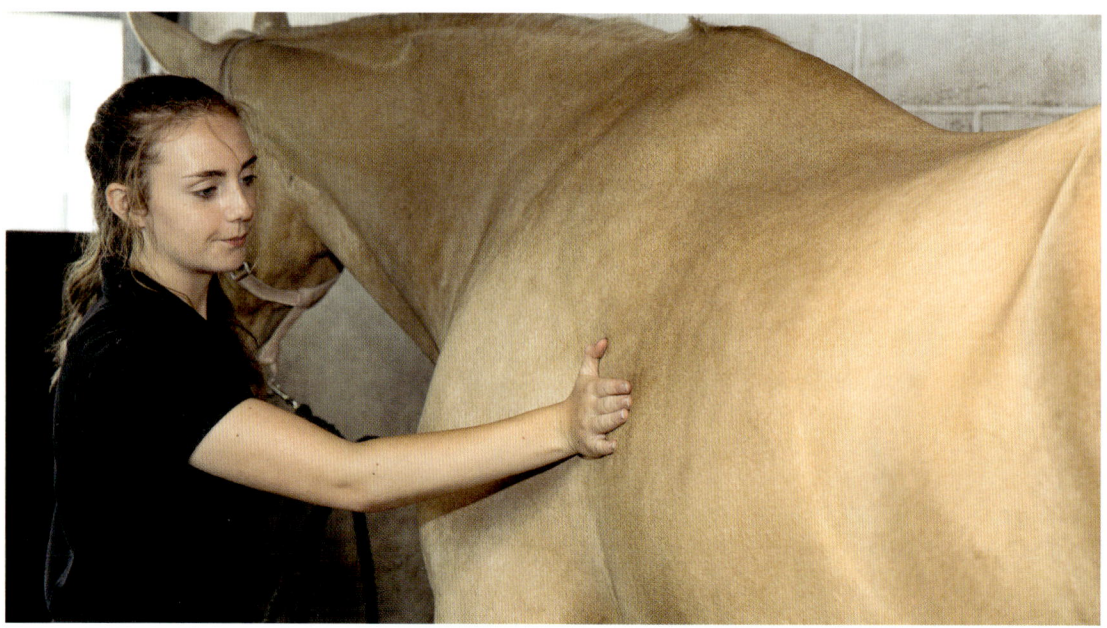

It is beneficial to do some training from the ground so that the horse moves over when asked. This can be started by getting the horse used to moving away from you in the stable.

Tying up

There may be times, such as on a picnic ride, when it is necessary to tie up horses while on a ride, so they must learn to stand quietly while tied for as long necessary. Whenever you ride out, always make sure that you have with you enough pieces of baling twine that can be split into strands that will break in an emergency if a horse suddenly pulls back. Make sure that you always tie horses with a lead rope attached to the headcollar – never be tempted to attach a lead rope to a bridle, as this can cause injury if the horse pulls back – and always use a quick-release knot so that you can release a horse quickly if you need to in an emergency.

Using saddlebags

If you are going to be out for a long time or even overnight it may be necessary for you to take extra bags with you, but it is a good idea to acclimatise horses to wearing a saddlebag before you set off. Initially, make sure that you place the bag gently across the horse's back and walk him round until he is used to the sensation. When he accepts this, put something in it – preferably something that has some weight and substance to it and even makes a noise – so that the horse becomes used to the sound.

If you are planning to do a long-distance ride (especially if this includes an overnight stay) you may wish to acclimatise your horse to wearing saddle bags.

Acclimatising horses to water

Horses used for riding out need to accept the fact that they are going to have to get their feet wet and muddy (in some areas, pretty frequently) so they need to be familiar with these scenarios before being ridden out by clients. (It would be ludicrous to expect a novice client to try to ride an unwilling or frightened horse through a significant water obstacle.) To introduce a horse to water, always choose somewhere that has shallow water with good footing for your first attempt, and be prepared with a headcollar and long rope in case you have to dismount and lead him across it to start with. Allow plenty of time and allow him to look at the water and

Riding Out

sniff it if he wants to. When he feels calm, gently ask him to walk forward, but be careful, as he may leap over or into it! As you repeat this exercise he will gradually get used to it and will tackle most such obstacles that he comes across on his travel.

Horses should be confident and happy to walk through water when being ridden by clients, so time should be taken in the horse's initial training to acclimatise them to this situation.

Fittening

In order to be ridden out for long distances, even if steadily and with breaks, the horses must be fit for the purpose. In general terms, the horses you are going to use will need to be fit enough to carry the riders for several hours at a time, maybe also with extra equipment, and to negotiate different types of terrain. Getting to this level involves a slow beginning, followed by a steady build-up of distances ridden, and later, gradual increases in speed, relevant to the work being done. Working horses further or faster than they can cope with, too soon, and too often, will almost always lead to injury.

The most important thing to bear in mind is that you need to start from a good foundation. Before beginning your fittening programme you will need to check that feet, teeth and general condition of the horses are satisfactory. Although these points are common requirements of all the horses, remember that each horse is an individual and should be treated as one, so you may need to adapt your programme accordingly. One point relating to individuality is that, while most horses require a visit from the farrier approximately every six weeks, this can't be assumed to apply to every horse. Some horses wear their shoes out more quickly than others, and some may have foot issues that require extra attention or non-standard shoeing. Therefore, the feet of all horses should be checked regularly between booked visits by the farrier to make sure that hooves or shoes don't require attention sooner. This reduces the danger of slipping or tripping out hacking, especially on uneven ground.

What follows is a general framework for a fittening programme.

Timescales for training

The time it takes for various body tissues to adapt and condition from the starting point of being unfit are as follows:

1. Heart and lungs   3 months
2. Muscles   3–6 months
3. Tendons and ligaments   6–12 months
4. Hooves   7 months
5. Bone   1–3 years

Phase 1 of the fittening programme

Aims

1. To prepare the horse physically and psychologically for more intensive exercise.
2. To start the conditioning of the legs and tendons.
3. To build muscle.
4. To render the horse calm and obedient.
5. To accustom the horse to hacking out.

For the starting point of the horse being unfit, hack him out four or five times each week for up to six weeks, gradually building up to 2–3 hours of active walk per session. During these sessions, he must walk with purpose and not lag, but also be walking properly, not jogging. He should learn to walk on a loose rein with his head down and neck extended so that his back can swing freely to develop the back muscles. It is a good idea to ride over varied terrain wherever possible – rough, stony tracks, ridges or hills, sand, and some roadwork for limited distances.

Riding Out

Walking on a loose rein with the head down and neck extended enables the horse's back to swing freely, which will help develop the back muscles.

During the early weeks of these work sessions only walk – the horse can trot on the lunge, and trot and canter during schooling in an arena, but during the work sessions the horse may only walk, even up hills. However, in the last two weeks of this programme, it is a good idea to introduce some trotting for short distances.

As walking is such low-intensity work, a rest day is not essential, but it will certainly do the fittening programme no harm to give the horse an occasional day off.

Phase 2 of the fittening programme

Aims

1. To develop the horse's stamina so that he can trot long distances rhythmically and at a constant speed.

2. To develop the trotting muscles and teach the horse an energy-saving trot.

3. To teach the horse not just to canter at random, but to stay in trot until asked to canter.

4. To prepare the horse physically for more intensive exercise.

In addition to starting some light schooling on some days, ride the horse out three or four times per week. Start out at walk until the horse is thoroughly warmed up (15–20 minutes). Then begin trotting slowly and alternate this with periods of walking if the horse becomes tired or out of breath. Build up gradually until the horse can trot on and off actively for up to 2 hours. A younger or less experienced horse should complete this phase more gradually than an experienced horse who is returning to fitness for the season. The horse must learn to trot in a relaxed manner with his head low, neck extended and back rounded so that he can develop long, powerful strides.

In this phase of the fittening process, it is important for the horse to have at least one rest day per week.

Phase 3 of the fittening programme

Aims

1. To increase fitness of the horse's heart and lungs.

2. To teach the horse to canter rhythmically and at a constant speed.

In addition to gradually increasing other work, introduce faster work sessions on rides out by incorporating approximately two sessions per week (or five sessions in 14 days). Make sure that you warm up the horse thoroughly before starting the faster work, and then introduce some trotting and cantering for short distances, alternating the two gaits to allow for short recovery sessions. At this point, introducing some hill work will help both fitness and balance. Build this work up gradually until the horse can trot and canter for a significant portion of a 2-hour ride without become overstressed. Longer rides can be undertaken at this point. It is important that the horse learns to canter at a controlled speed with other horses.

Incorporating hill work increases fitness and balance.

Riding Out

Lungeing can be used as part of the fittening programme.

Summary

- Build the horse up gradually to maximum work.

- A stressful session must be followed by a day of recovery.

- As you train faster and harder, you need to put in more recovery days. While you are just walking, no days for recovery are necessary, but you need to lunge and school to develop the horse properly.

- Remember that the principle of improvement is based on stress and recovery to a higher plane of fitness. If no recovery is allowed, you will break down what you have built up by causing injuries to the weakest parts.

- No more than two of the hardest workouts per week.

- Don't do hard workouts on consecutive days.

- One complete rest day per week.

- Lunge one day a week, working on a slow, rhythmic trot for around 20 minutes as this will improve obedience, suppleness and power.

- One day a week, school the horse under saddle to make him supple and obedient.

TRAINING TIPS

1. It is a good idea to keep track of the exercise regime for all the horses on the yard.

2. Learn how to take a horse's pulse and do so regularly before exercise (a typical resting pulse should be 28–44). After exercise take the pulse again, and repeat 10 minutes after stopping exercise, to see how quickly the pulse drops. The fitter the horse, the faster it should return to the normal resting rate for that horse.

Chapter 6

Allocating Horses to Riders

Horse hours

Weight-carrying ability

Assessing clients prior to riding out

Summary

Allocating Horses to Riders

Horse hours

Attempting the most appropriate match-up of horses and riders is an important matter for all parties concerned, but the availability of suitable horses at any particular time is fundamental to this. In this respect, one important consideration is that the horses available should be neither overworked nor, indeed, underworked to the extent that they are insufficiently fit, or over-fresh.

Trying to give guidance on precisely how many hours per day or week any individual horse can be used is very difficult as there are so many factors to be taken in to consideration. However, those to bear in mind include:

- Age
- Type/breed
- Fitness level
- Intensity of the session
- Terrain (surface)
- Weather conditions and temperature
- Experience of the rider

Further to this last point, there are various factors to consider. If a horse is used primarily as a sightseeing conveyance for very inexperienced riders, he will not be working in the sense that experienced riders would understand but, as mentioned shortly, inexperienced riders will often 'ride heavier' than an experienced rider of the same weight. On the other hand, experienced riders will often expect to do more fast work and will be happy to confront more challenging terrain (e.g. steep hills) than would be the case with those less experienced.

Another point to bear in mind when allocating hours is that, if a horse is healthy, regular work of suitable intensity is beneficial – but an eye should be kept on total 'work hours'. For example, it's unfair to overwork a horse because he's a 'client favourite'.

Weight-carrying ability

This is an issue for equine welfare and one that the BHS considers to be so important that they are helping to fund research into this topic through The Animal Health Trust. *Please note that the percentages provided below, although current, will be subject to change once the research has been concluded and are for guidance only*. That said, the general policy of the BHS regarding rider's weight is clear:

1. No horse should be asked to carry more weight than he is able to do comfortably. Failure to adhere to this is a breach of welfare and may cause long-term physiological damage to the animal.

2. Riding is an inclusive sport and has many physical and health benefits for the rider. There is a suitable horse for almost everyone who is within a healthy weight range for their height. However, any particular horse must be chosen carefully to match the intended rider and riders must accept that there are some horses who are not sufficiently robust to carry them safely. Some riding establishments may not have horses large enough to carry riders over a certain weight and in these circumstances a rider will need to look elsewhere for riding opportunities.

The question of precisely how much weight an individual horse can carry safely is regularly asked of the BHS. Unfortunately there is a dearth of robust and reliable peer-reviewed research on the subject, which thus remains subjective rather than being firmly based on science, and it is therefore not possible for the BHS to produce definitive figures. However, the points below set out the recommendations of the society and will be reviewed and revised as research develops.

In simple terms and in most circumstances the BHS recommends that a horse or pony is regularly asked to carry no more than:

- 10 per cent of his ideal bodyweight if performing at an extremely high intensity (e.g. elite competition).

- 18 per cent of his ideal bodyweight in other circumstances.

These figures are not inclusive of the horse's tack, and allowances should be made if the horse is required to wear unusually heavy tack. It is essential that these calculations are based on *ideal* rather than *actual* bodyweight of the horse. A horse who is significantly overweight will not be sufficiently fit to carry 18 per cent of his obese bodyweight. A horse who is significantly underweight should not be ridden at all.

There are, however, a number of factors that must be taken into consideration when determining the maximum weight that a horse should be asked to carry. These factors have some parallels to the work hours mentioned above, and include (but are not limited to) the following:

Age

It is not possible to prescribe definite weight limits according to the age of the horse as fitness and experience are equally important. Additionally cold-blooded breeds (such as the Irish Draught) will tend to mature more slowly than warm and hot-blooded breeds such as the Thoroughbred. However, it is generally a likelihood that young horses may not have developed sufficient balance and musculature to carry a full 18% of their ideal bodyweight.

At the other end of the age spectrum, elderly horses should also not be expected to carry a full 18% of their ideal bodyweight because of the effects of age and wear and tear on the body. The age at which a horse should be considered as 'elderly' will vary with the fitness of the horse in question.

Breed

Certain breeds have been developed specifically to carry weight. The Highland Pony, as an example, was in part developed in order to transport heavy deer carcasses at a slow and steady pace. It would therefore be realistic to expect animals of this type to carry rather more than

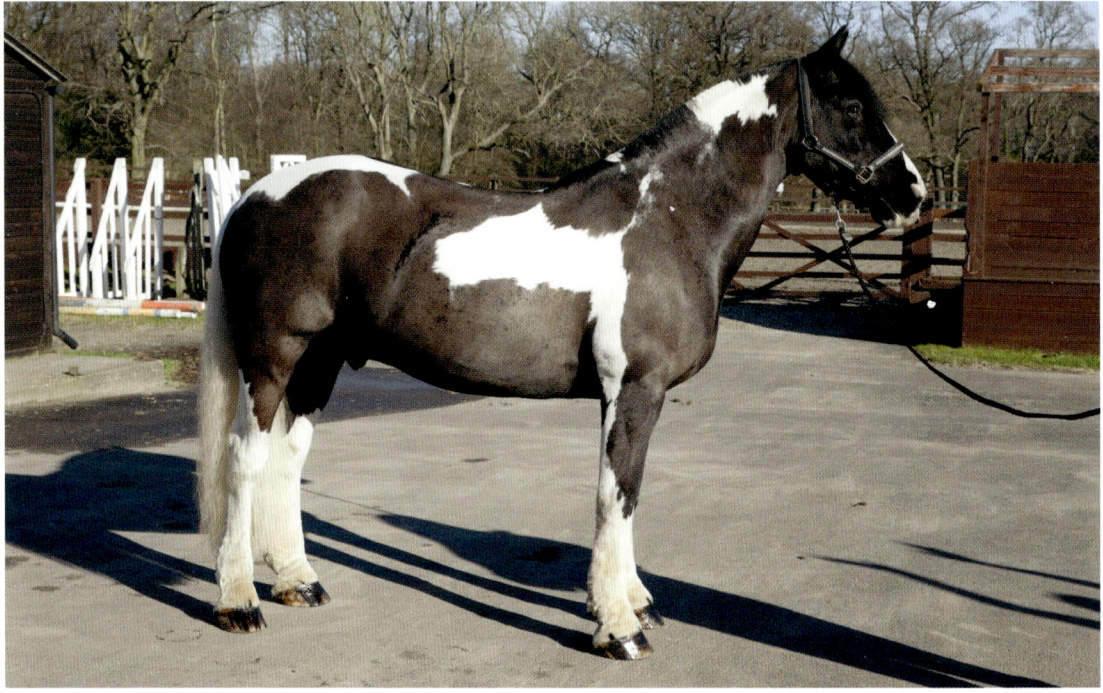

It is practical to have horses who can carry a variety of riders of different weights at trekking centres.

6 | Allocating Horses to Riders

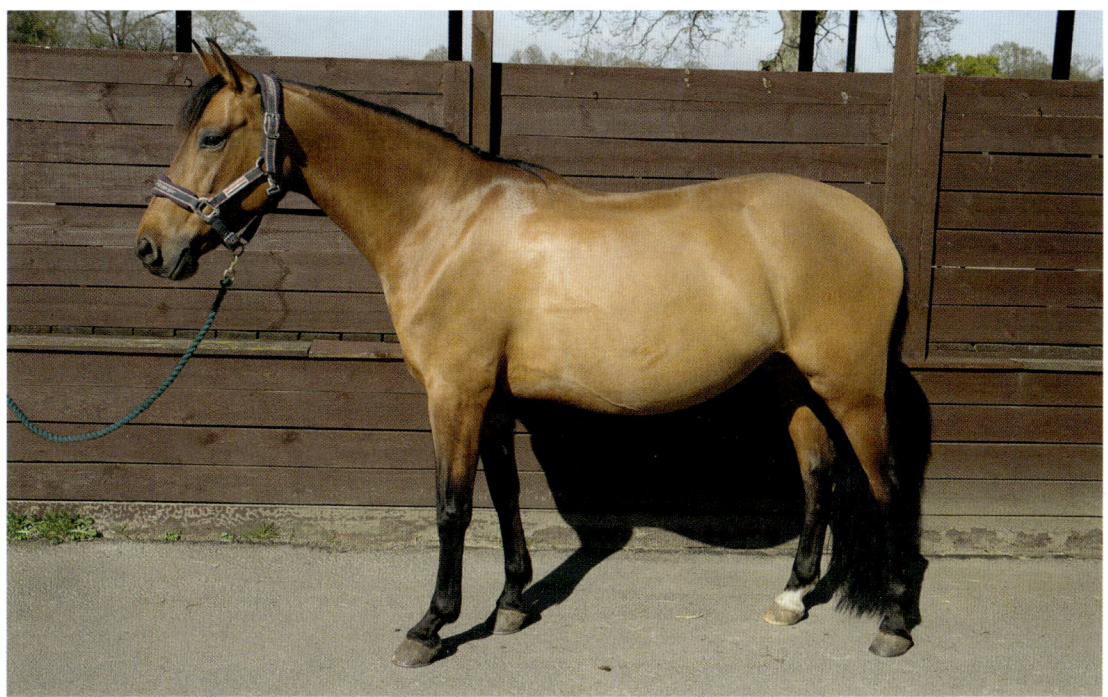

Whilst this pony would be suitable for children and a lightweight adult, he would not be suitable for taller or larger adults.

the recommended limit of 18% of ideal bodyweight assuming that there are no compounding factors and that relatively slow work is being performed.

Conformation

There is often a close correlation between a horse's conformation and his breed, but this cannot be guaranteed and it is therefore always important to assess each individual. The conformation of a horse's back is particularly important in determining the maximum weight he can carry. Irregularities in the shape of the spine, such as sway backs and pronounced withers (particularly common in older horses), mechanically weaken the spine and limit weight-carrying capacity.

Another important factor in weight-carry capacity is the quality and amount of 'bone' a horse has – the amount being a measurement of the circumference of the limb below the knee around the canon bone including the soft tissue (i.e. tendons and ligaments). Mechanically, the canon bones can be thought of as 'pillars' that help to support the horse, so a horse with substantial bone will be physically stronger in this respect than one 'lacking in bone'.

Just as strong limbs will enhance a horse's weight-carrying capacity, any limb deformities will reduce or compromise it, and possibly have an adverse effect on his balance.

There are many other conformational and postural faults that may affect a horse's weight-carrying ability and some of these may counter strengths in other areas. If there is any concern about a horse's conformation, the advice of an expert should be sought.

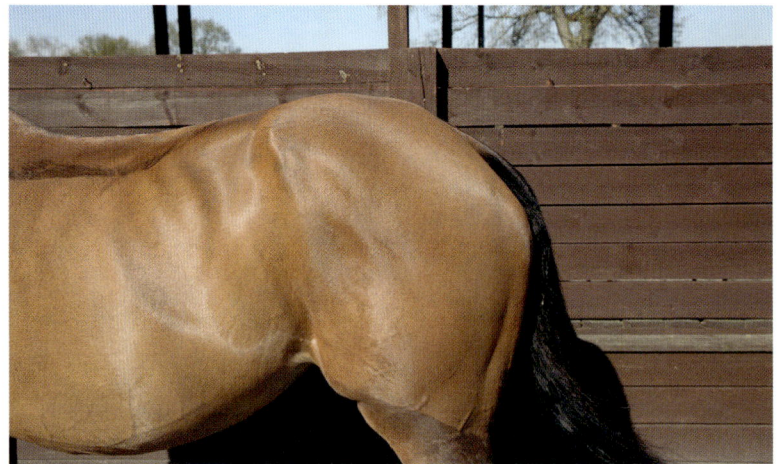

This horse has a slightly sway back, which can limit weight-carrying capacity.

Fitness

A horse may be at his ideal weight without necessarily being that physically fit. Likewise, a horse may be ridden frequently but if that riding consists primarily of low-intensity work he will not be at peak fitness. An unfit horse should not be asked to carry as much weight as one who has, through controlled and regular exercise, developed the musculature of a fit horse. (*See* also previous chapter.)

Type, frequency and duration of work to be undertaken

It is important to consider whether it is fair to expect a horse to carry his maximum load on a very regular basis, particularly if he is working at a high intensity or for long periods. Particular consideration should be given in the case of a novice or inexperienced rider, who may ride 'heavier' than an experienced rider of the same weight (*see* below). Furthermore, regardless of the intensity of the work, riding centres should ensure that their horses are not consistently working at the limit of their weight-carrying abilities.

To put matters of weight into perspective, the frequency and intensity of the work expected of horses working at exceptionally high levels, i.e. elite competition horses, means that they should carry only 10 per cent of their ideal bodyweight.

Rider's ability

A beginner or novice rider is unlikely to have developed sufficient balance and skill to prevent them from moving around in the saddle. This will have a negative impact on the horse's spine. With experience come balance and poise, which ease the burden on the horse. It is likely that a horse will find a 76kg (12st) well-balanced experienced rider easier to carry than a 63.5kg (10st) novice who does not yet have the skill to remain stable in the saddle. A common issue with learner riders is the tendency to lean forwards. The horse at rest carries 60 per cent of his bodyweight on his forelimbs (in part because of the length and weight of the head and neck) so the addition of weight on the forehand from an unbalanced rider is not conducive to the long-term integrity of the forelimb structures. Of course, it is recognised that every rider needs to learn, but the suggestion is that, until they have a secure seat, they are restricted to horses for whom the rider's weight equates to less than 18 per cent of the horse's bodyweight.

It is hoped that the factors mentioned will be useful in determining the practical weight-carrying ability of individual horses but, in instances where this is in doubt expert advice should be sought. BHS Accredited Professional Coaches will be able to offer impartial and honest guidance.

The British Horse Society firmly believes that almost everyone can find a horse that can carry them safely. Riders who weigh more may need to invest some time and effort in finding a horse that will meet their needs. Under no circumstances should the welfare of a horse be compromised by the weight of its rider. There will be occasions when BHS Approved Riding Schools will not be able to accommodate clients due to their weight. The BHS supports the schools' decisions but will be happy to assist riders to find an approved riding school that does meet their needs.

Assessing clients prior to riding out

Before you take a group of riders out, you must be confident that they are capable and safe on the horses they are riding. It is always a good idea to see new clients in an enclosed arena for a short time so that you can assess their level of competence, make sure that they are mounted appropriately and form an opinion about whether you may need to modify your intended route or the speed of the ride.

As mentioned in Chapter 3, new clients should ideally have completed a questionnaire outlining their riding ability, so you should have a basic idea of the standard of riding to expect but, beware, people do not always have the same opinion of their riding ability as you might!

Especially if you have clients visiting from abroad (the USA in particular), if you only use English tack, it is worth checking that they have had experience of riding in English tack, as the technique for riding in Western style can be a very different skill. (Of course, if yours is one of the UK centres that offers Western-style riding, the converse applies – you should ask visiting clients whether they have had previous experience of this style.)

Western tack

*If your centre uses Western tack, and it is likely that many of your clients will be unfamiliar with it, it is worth bearing in mind the following. These points may also help highlight some differences that clients who **normally** ride Western-style will encounter if your centre uses English tack.*

- *Western saddles are usually heavier than their English counterparts, and this should be borne in mind when assessing the weight-carrying capacity of horses used for Western riding.*

- *Cinches (Western girths) can take longer than English ones to tighten, and this can't usually be done from the saddle, so there is a time factor to be borne in mind when dealing with a group of riders. If the saddle is fitted with a flank cinch then this must be attached to the front cinch with a joining strap in the middle of the belly line – otherwise if can act as a 'bucking strap'.*

- *Western stirrups can come in a variety of shapes and sizes, but it is still important that they are the correct size for the rider's feet. The wrong size can be awkward, uncomfortable, distracting and painful – and will certainly compromise the rider's safety. Similarly to English stirrups, Western stirrups should have about a finger's width of room on each side of the foot. This will allow enough play and freedom of movement without the foot slipping about or becoming wedged. (Endurance riders may opt for stirrups that are extra-wide across the base of the foot, as these are specially designed for maximum weight distribution.)*

- *When dismounting, Western-style riders normally step down with their left foot still in the stirrup. This is partly because the construction of a Western saddle makes it difficult for a rider to lean forward in the conventional English style. It does, however, carry the risk that, if the horse moves off suddenly during the dismount, the rider's foot could be caught in the stirrup. Therefore, due vigilance is necessary if this style is being used. Also, be mindful that a client used to riding Western style might do this instinctively if riding in English tack.*

- *Western bridles are of a rather different pattern from English ones and, while a rider who is fairly experienced with one type will probably be able to fit the other type fairly readily, this can't be assumed, and less experienced riders from one style shouldn't be expected to fit the other without supervision.*

- *Western tack often incorporates curb bits with long shanks. These can be used with the utmost delicacy by experienced practitioners, but have the potential to cause damage in the hands of an inexperienced novice – especially one who is nervous or unbalanced. Holiday riding centres may find it preferable to use snaffle bits (which are also employed in some forms of Western riding). If these are fitted to Western-style bridles, be mindful that such bridles rarely have the same capacity for adjustment as English ones, so it is important that they are chosen to be a good fit for the individual horse. (Bosals and hackamores might also be usefully employed for hacking.)*

- *Classical Western riding involves using split reins (i.e. not joined together), which are held in one hand; directional rein aids are given by neck-reining. Both these features will be unfamiliar to clients who have only previously ridden English style (and, of course, vice versa). While experienced riders in either style will probably 'get' and adapt to the different style fairly quickly (and enjoy the challenge), novice riders who are just coming to terms with one method may find the change initially confusing. Where it is likely that newcomers to Western will be novices whose experience is of English style, it might be preferable to use joined reins in conjunction with snaffle bridles. Riding centres should, of course, ensure that their horses are well schooled to respond to the aiding methods used.*

- *When riding at the faster gaits in Western tack, because of the different style of saddle, there will be less modification of the seat than is seen in the English form of forward seat. Further to this, the gaits of jog and lope used in Western riding are not truly commensurate with the English rising trot and canter, so it doesn't really work to combine the two styles on the same ride out.*

- *There are some differences of terminology between English and Western riding, and it may be interesting for riders from either style to learn the alternatives. However, significant changes should be signalled in advance of being given as commands – for example, those used to English terminology may be baffled by being told, out of the blue, that the ride is about to 'lope'.*

- *In Western style, riders do not traditionally wear hard hats. However, centres with BHS approved status for riding out should ensure that this is done.*

Categories of riders

The following broad categories of riders will give you an approximate idea of what you *should* be able to expect from information provided on client questionnaires, but you will need to make your own judgement in the light of what you see during the ridden assessment.

Total beginners have little (if any) experience at all with horses in general. A beginner may have been on a 'holiday hack' once or twice but may not know how to move forward, turn, trot, canter and stop unassisted. They cannot lead, groom, or tack up a horse and may not be comfortable handling a horse on the ground.

Advanced beginners have a little experience with horses. They may have grown up around horses or taken a few lessons, but are not confident enough to tack up a horse. Such riders can mount and walk unassisted. They can ask the horse to move forward, turn and stop. They may be able to rise to the trot on a very smooth, well-trained horse.

Confident beginners have the knowledge of an advanced beginner, but will also be able to handle a horse who is less willing to do as asked. These riders have the confidence to give a little kick if needed, or use a more persuasive aid when required, even though they may lack experience. They should be quite confident in rising trot and are able to canter on a smooth, comfortable obliging horse.

Novice riders have had a few lessons, may have owned a horse as a child, but have not competed or trained young, green horses. They can catch, groom, and may be able to tack up a horse. They can change direction and ride a circle as well as having a basic understanding of what a diagonal is and what leads are. They may even have started a little jumping and are comfortable on a quiet well-schooled horse, but may not be comfortable on a greener, younger or less experienced mount.

Intermediate riders have taken lessons or trained with an instructor or coach for a while, and may compete at a low level. They will have ridden several different types of horses and can independently manage a horse's care. Their seat is pretty secure, they rarely lose balance and, on any occasion when they do, they are likely to regain it with minimal disturbance to the horse. They know how to ask for and obtain a specific lead or change of lead. They are capable of riding a less experienced horse and helping in that horse's training.

Advanced riders have ridden most of their lives and have worked with a trainer/mentor for several years, or had several years with intense riding instruction. They have competed successfully at recognised shows in their discipline. They are able to ride most horses, including working with young/green horses without assistance. They know advanced manoeuvres in their preferred riding discipline and can positively affect the horse they are riding at all times. Advanced riders are able to back and train horses, give lessons to beginners and teach a horse advanced manoeuvres. They know horse breeds and conformation well and are able to detect unsoundness and recognise blemishes in a horse.

Preliminaries

Tack checks

Before you mount your riders to assess their level of competence, it is vitally important to check that the tack on the horses you are planning to take out for a ride is safe for use. Ideally it should all be checked on a regular basis and it can be most convenient to do this while it is being cleaned. The main areas to check are the stirrup leathers, girth straps, reins and cheekpieces.

It is also important to be aware of the fit of the tack, as horses may change shape through the season as they become fitter or lose weight as they are working harder. Try to look for any signs that the tack is not comfortable for the horse – such as the saddle pressing down on the withers or physical symptoms like the horse being unwilling to go forwards, swishing his tail or pulling faces when the girth is tightened. The weight of the rider can also affect the fit of the tack so it should be taken into consideration when the tack is fitted, especially if the horse is being expected to carry a rider towards the limit of his weight-carrying capacity.

Make sure that the numnah is big enough, that the front has been pulled up into the channel or gullet of the saddle to prevent pressure over the withers and that it has an attachment to secure it to the saddle, to help prevent movement and rucking.

Always make sure that the numnah is pulled up into the gullet to prevent pressure on the horse's withers.

You also need to check the girth straps under the saddle flaps to ensure that all straps and stitching are secure and that the bars that hold the stirrup leathers are undamaged and not turned up, so that the stirrup leathers can slide off in an emergency. The leathers themselves should be checked for wear and cracking. It is important to make sure that the stirrups are the correct size for the rider's feet, especially so if the rider is not wearing proper riding boots.

In addition to making sure that the stitching around the girth buckles is secure, you need to check that the buckles themselves are not damaged or bent and that the girth does not show signs of wear and tear.

When you are checking the bridle, look to see that none of the leather or synthetic material shows any signs of weakness, wear or cracking and that all the stitching is secure. It is particularly important to make sure that the stitching on the reins is sound and that the bit is the correct size and appropriate type for the horse's mouth, with no dirt or rough edges that may damage his mouth.

If possible, engage with the riders when checking tack. This can act as an 'ice-breaker' and may give an early clue to levels of experience. It is a good aim to have stirrups roughly pre-adjusted before moving the horse to the mounting block: although not entirely accurate, getting a rider to put their fingers at the top of the stirrup leather and measuring the length of the leather to the stirrup at their armpit is a good starting point, and a further opportunity for dialogue.

Initial observation of riders

One thing to check is what the riders are wearing. New clients should have been given advice about appropriate and inappropriate clothing at the time of their initial booking (*see* Liaising with Clients and Booking Procedure in Chapter 3), but this is the time to see whether they have taken the advice on board. In some instances, there may be an opportunity for a rider to change a particular item of clothing for something more suitable.

First, check how riders have put on their hats. Do they look correct and balanced, or are some hats resting to the side or on the back of heads? The latter may require that you suggest an adjustment. Observe straight away how clients conduct themselves around the horses. Are they able to lead the horse from the stable? Do they check their own tack? Can they tighten girths and adjust their stirrups?

Mounting

Watching riders mount and adjusting their equipment will tell you more about them. Are they able to mount unaided, or do they require guidance and help? A rider requiring help to mount and to make basic adjustments would indicate inexperience, while a rider who can quickly adjust their stirrups with their feet still placed in the irons while holding the reins to control the horse would indicate some experience.

If a rider is hunched over or tips forward as soon as the horse moves this may indicate experience and/or nervousness.

Riders may not all sit in a perfect position, but if they are sitting easily in the saddle and look confident, they probably have sufficient experience for hacking.

Once riders are mounted, guide them if necessary into the right position and explain why. Although it is not always possible to get an ideal saddle fit for every rider, they should be reasonably comfortable. The old adage 'sit in the deepest part of the saddle' remains good advice, and should be encouraged and explained. From there, show them how to drop their legs down with knees bent and lift their toes up to place their feet in the stirrups. They should be encouraged to sit up in order to balance over their legs. Check the position of the riders' legs and, if necessary, help them to position their legs into the right place, resting just behind the girth with the lower legs bent slightly back from the knee. It is always difficult to determine precisely how long a rider's stirrup leathers should be. However, remember that, after the initial assessment, these riders will not be riding in a school environment but outside with the need, on occasions, get into a forward position. Therefore the length of leg should be sufficient to provide support, but not so short as to push them onto the back of the saddle or making rising trot difficult. When riders are about to ride out on possibly uneven terrain, if they initially feel a little 'between holes' on the leathers, they are usually better opting for the 'shorter' holes.

Riding Out

If it is necessary to tell riders how to hold the reins, show three fingers over the reins and the little finger below. The thumb sits on top of the loose part of the rein.

Although riding in a perfect position is not required, a rider who sits easily in the saddle, holding their reins correctly and looking ready for the off is probably fairly experienced. Riders who are very tense, hunched over, clasping at the reins nervously and/or tipping forward as soon as the horse moves, are indicating a lack of experience.

The assessment session

When you assess a group of riders prior to taking them out, it is worth remembering that some of them see this as a fairly pointless, time-wasting exercise. It is therefore important that you use your skills to decide fairly quickly and efficiently whether they are up to the standard that you require for the level of hack you are planning. Also, an individual may be basically competent, but their riding style may not suit a particular horse so bear that in mind and be prepared to swap the horse if necessary.

Remember that you are not there to coach for a dressage test or jump a course of showjumps – your priorities are to ensure that they are safe and in control for the level of hack envisaged.

It is essential that new clients are assessed before leaving for a ride out. They must be safe and in control of the horse they are riding.

When you have checked that all girths are tight and stirrups are of a suitable length, send the ride out in an enclosed area in walk. Confirm that they are able to steer, turn both ways and halt on command. With very novice riders, it may be necessary to explain basic control of the horse; the use of the reins, right and left, stopping and starting. Most riders will understand the basic concepts of pressure and release, which should be explained simply, along the following lines. To stop or slow, increased pressure of the reins, accompanied by relaxation of pressure from the legs. To go forward, or increase speed, increased pressure from the legs, accompanied by a reduction of the pressure on the reins. To turn, the rein in the direction of the turn is opened (moved outward – not pulled back) while the pressure on the opposite rein is reduced slightly. At the same time, the rider's leg on the side of the turn presses on the girth, while the leg on the opposite side is moved back a little to rest against the horse's side.

It is a natural reaction for most novice riders to grip with their legs, this should be discouraged with due explanation as some horses may take it as a signal to go faster. Also, of course, such gripping up actually *reduces* the security of the seat and a horse speeding up while the rider is getting more insecure is a scenario to be avoided.

If the riders show that they can cope readily with basic manoeuvres in walk, the next stage is to ask them to repeat them in trot. If necessary, assist them to prepare to trot by ensuring that their reins are of a suitable length and held in both hands. They should ask the horse to trot with their legs and be ready to move forward to rising trot straight away. If in any doubt, encourage riders to use their neckstraps as, if they pull back on the reins, their horses will be reluctant to move forward. Tell riders to move forward and rise gently from the saddle. It helps if there is a slight forward inclination from the hips as they rise from the saddle.

If the ride is going to involve faster work you will need to see riders in canter.

When you are satisfied that your riders are safe and in control you must decide the preferred order that they will ride in when you go out – although as we shall see in Chapter 8, there might sometimes be a need to rethink this. You will then need to go over any instructions for procedures relative to your route before setting off with your ride.

Summary

- Have a session where all horses and ponies are put on a weigh bridge (many veterinary practices offer this service free of charge) so that you know whether they are over- or underweight.

- Make sure that each horse has a profile that indicates the size and type of rider that is suitable for him.

- Encourage clients to be honest about their riding ability when they book.

Riding Out

- Read the centre registration form before you start so that you have an idea of the level of riding ability to expect.

- Make sure that you check the fit and comfort of the tack before you ask riders to mount.

- Check the hat standards and that each hat is fitted correctly to the rider.

- Make sure that you are friendly and encouraging throughout the process – regardless of the level of rider!

TRAINING TIPS

1. Learn how to 'condition score' a horse so that you know that all animals are in top condition for the work they will be asked to do.

2. Practise assessing riders who are not known to you so you become used to categorising their ability in your head.

3. If riders are competent in walk, watch them going into trot so that you can assess them. They should adapt to a rising trot with a slight inclination forward in the upper body without falling back heavily into the saddle or pulling back on the reins.

4. Likewise when they move into canter (if appropriate) they should look forward to ask the horse confidently to canter and remain in balance without falling back or tipping forward.

5. Look for riders to be confident when using leg and rein aids; they should be clear but not rough.

6. Look for the levels of confidence in control of the horses and balance of riders when determining the style of ride being undertaken.

Chapter 7

Useful Skills and Knowledge for Planning Rides

Map-reading skills and GPS

Riding on the road

Basic understanding of the countryside

Risk-assessing the planned route

Summary

Useful Skills and Knowledge for Planning Rides

Thoughtful planning and preparation are key to maximising the success of any ride out, and are especially crucial in respect of long rides (e.g. perhaps with overnight stops), rides across challenging terrain and, indeed, those involving unfamiliar clients of perhaps limited experience.

Map-reading skills and GPS

This knowledge is a great asset for anyone planning riding routes and may, on occasion, be very useful during the course of a ride – particularly a longer one in a relatively new area, or if problems are encountered during the ride. In general terms, improving your map-reading skills will increase your hacking potential in most areas. Feeling comfortable with maps will help you to enjoy a far greater range of places to ride, to feel secure in knowing where you are in relation to the map, and how far you can go in how much time. The Ordnance Survey (OS) produces superb maps and excellent guides on how to read them. The best for riders is the 1:25,000 Explorer map (orange cover), which is available on paper or for various GPS and smartphone apps. You can also see it online at www.streetmap.co.uk and www.magic.gov.uk.

Reading a map

When you look at a map, study the map key (which will be printed usually in one corner) and note the line styles for bridleways, byways ('restricted byway' and 'byway open to all traffic') and 'other routes with public access' (*see also* further information on these terms later in this chapter). Some people like to highlight the useable routes on the map in their area to make it easier to see at a glance. There may also be permissive bridleways marked, and many routes described in the key as 'traffic-free cycle routes' are open to horses, and there may be other places where you can ride depending on location and local landowners.

(A cautionary note here: if you have to consult a paper map while out riding, don't attempt to do so from the saddle – dismount and, if possible, ask someone else to hold your horse.)

Grid references

When you go out hacking it is important that you know how to read coordinates on the map so that you know where you are if you need to inform anyone such as the emergency services. You can do this by looking at grid references. This is one of the most important map-reading skills, because you can pinpoint any specific location on a map.

Looking at any OS map, you will see that it is divided into squares by vertical and horizontal lines. The physical size of the squares *on the map* will vary depending on the scale of the map – for example, on an Explorer map, the squares are 4×4cm while, on a Landranger map (pink cover), they are 2×2cm. In each case, however, one square represents 1km² – the sort of total area that an average sized village might cover although, of course, villages are rarely square!

The lines that create the squares are numbered with 2-digit numbers as follows.

- The numbers of the *vertical lines* increase as the lines move across the map from left to right, which represents from west to east. Because of this, these lines are called *eastings*.

- The numbers of the *horizontal lines* increase as the lines move up the map from bottom to top, which represents from south to north. Because of this, these lines are called *northings*.

The number of every line appears at both ends of the line, on the edges of the map, for convenience of reference. For example, if you are looking at a feature near the top right of a map, it is easier to check the numbers on the top right borders than to start running a finger down or across the whole map.

Map extract.

A basic (4-digit) grid reference for any square on the map can be given by stating the *easting* number for the line on *the left edge* of that square, followed by the *northing* number *along the bottom edge* of the square. Using the map extract illustration (*see* previous page) you will see that the village of Plaitford in the top right-hand (north-eastern) corner has a grid reference of 2719. (The reference always has to be in the order of *easting* followed by *northing* and it is important to think left side; bottom of square, otherwise an incorrect reference will result.)

While a four-figure reference may be sufficient (if, for example, you *do* just want to locate a village), there may be times when it is useful, or important, to be more precise. You might, for example, want to pinpoint a post office or pub or, more crucially, provide coordinates for the emergency services if someone is injured. To do this, you can work out a 6-figure reference that will pinpoint location to within about one-hundredth of a km^2, by dividing the main square in which the feature lies into a hundred little ones.

To use another example from the map illustration, if you look at the square with the grid reference 2619 to the south-west of Plaitford, you will see a small pond (the blue blob). Referring to the 2-digit *easting* line (26), you will see that the pond is about four-tenths of the way further right (east) of that line, so you add a 4 after the 26, making the precise *easting* 264. Then, looking up from the *northing* line (19), you will see that the pond is (about) three-tenths of the way further up (north) of that line, so you add 3 after the 19, making 193. Remembering that you always quote the whole *eastings* number first, you now have a 6-digit grid reference of 264193.

In addition to numbered grid lines, OS maps have codes consisting of two letters, which can be found printed in faint blue capitals. The whole of Great Britain is divided into squares of 100km and each square is given two letters. There will be a diagram within your map's key showing you which areas of the map fall into which squares of the National Grid. When you quote your six-digit grid reference you should put the two letters of the area you are in before the numbers. This means that there is no doubt or confusion about your location.

Basic symbols

There are some basic features that most maps will include. Roads tend to be marked in different colours depending on the type of road depicted, ranging from thick blue lines showing motorways, to dashed lines, indicating an unfenced minor road.

Footpaths are marked on OS maps in various colours. On a 1:25 000 scale OS Explorer Map the public rights of way are marked in green and on a 1:50 000 scale OS Landranger Map they are marked in magenta. There are various types of public rights of way and public access, so make sure you check the map key for full information. It is important to be aware that footpaths that are shown in black are not necessarily public rights of way.

7 | Useful Skills and Knowledge for Planning Rides

OS EXPLORER FLASHCARDS
Index 1 to 45

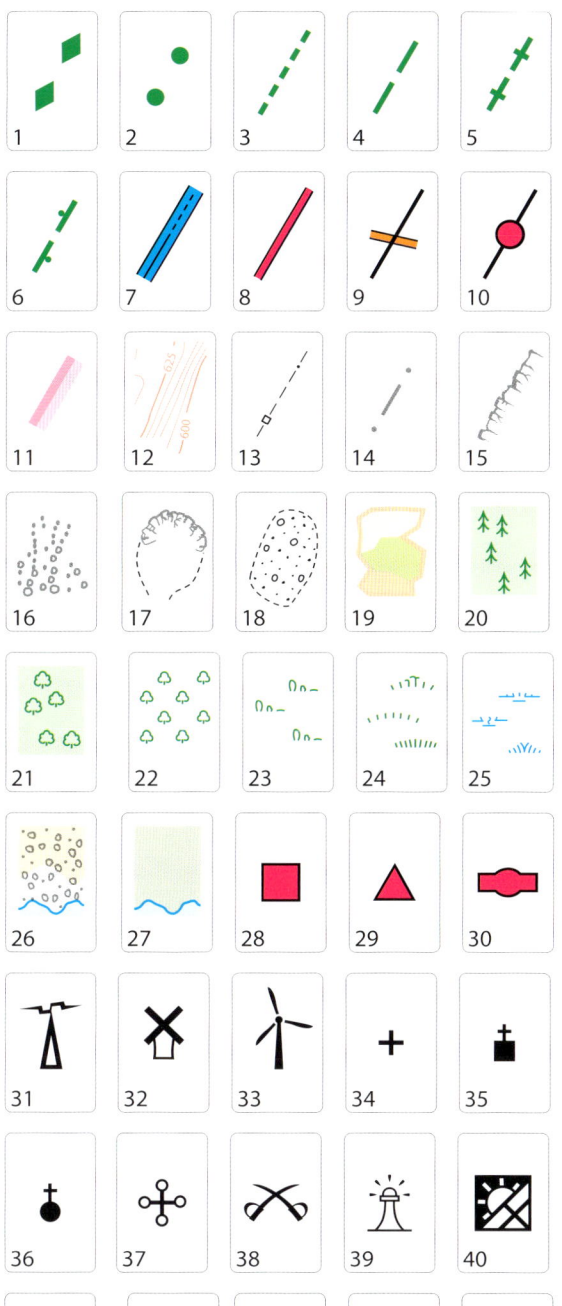

1. Recreational path
2. Other route with public access
3. Footpath
4. Bridleway
5. Byway open to all traffic
6. Restricted byway
7. Motorway
8. A road
9. Level crossing
10. Railway station
11. National Park boundary
12. Contours (5m interval)
13. Electricity transmission line
14. County boundary
15. Cliff
16. Scree
17. Quarry
18. Spoil heap
19. Access land
20. Coniferous wood
21. Non-coniferous wood
22. Orchard
23. Scrub
24. Bracken, heath or rough grassland
25. Marsh, reeds or saltings
26. Shingle
27. Mud
28. Bunkhouse, camping barn or other hostel
29. Youth hostel
30. Bus station
31. Mast
32. Windmill
33. Wind turbine
34. Place of worship
35. " – with tower
36. " – with spire or dome
37. Site of antiquity
38. Site of battle
39. Lighthouse
40. Solar farm
41. Camping and caravan site
42. Viewpoint (180°)
43. Parking
44. Information centre (seasonal)
45. Public phone

Riding Out

OS EXPLORER FLASHCARDS

Index 46 to 90

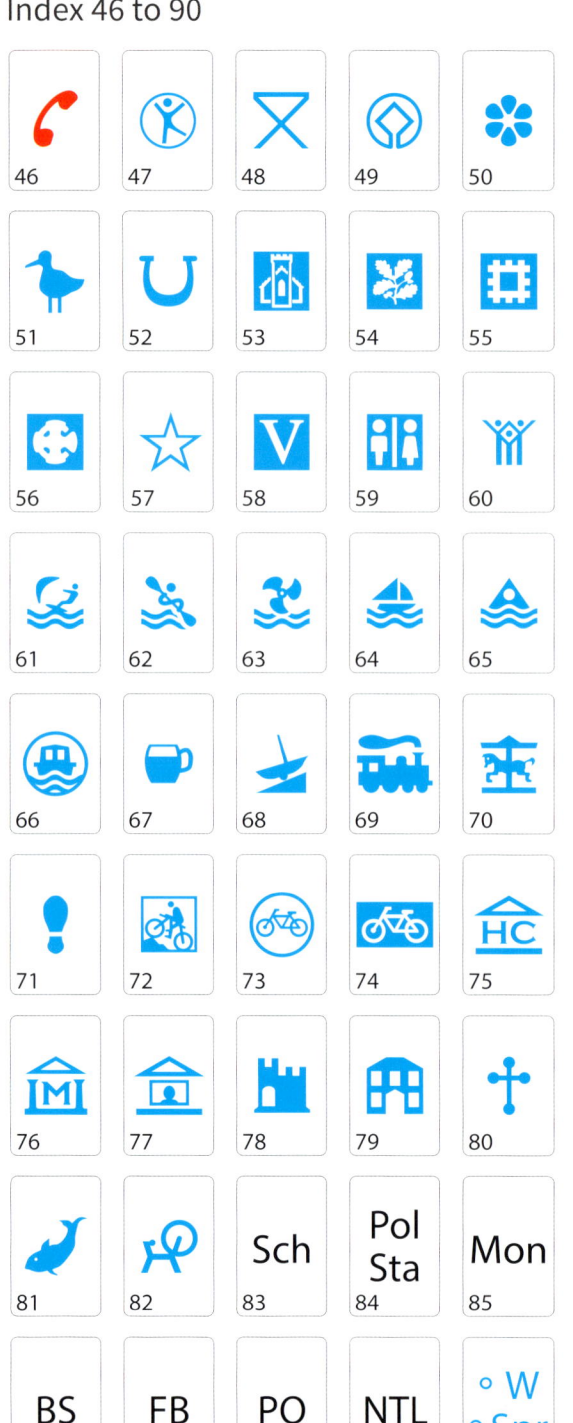

46	Emergency phone
47	Recreation, leisure or sports centre
48	Picnic site
49	World Heritage centre or area
50	Garden or arboretum
51	Nature reserve
52	Horse riding
53	Historic Scotland
54	National Trust
55	English Heritage
56	Welsh Heritage (CADW)
57	Other tourist feature
58	Visitor centre
59	Toilets
60	Country park
61	Water activities (board)
62	Water activities (paddle)
63	Water activities (powered)
64	Water activities (sailing)
65	Watersports centre (multi-activity)
66	Boat hire
67	Public house
68	Slipway
69	Preserved railway
70	Theme park
71	Walk or trail
72	Mountain bike trail
73	Bike hire
74	Cycle trail
75	Heritage centre
76	Museum
77	Art gallery
78	Castle
79	Historic house
80	Abbey or cathedral
81	Fishing
82	Craft centre
83	School
84	Police station
85	Monument
86	Boundary stone
87	Footbridge
88	Post Office
89	Normal Tidal Limit
90	Well, Spring

Woods are shown in green, with a coniferous or non-coniferous tree shape printed over the top, and buildings are marked by small black squares. However, some particular buildings have their own special symbols, such as churches and windmills. Any of these buildings can be useful landmarks, helping you to check your position on the map.

Rivers and streams are shown as blue lines. The width of the line is representative of the watercourse width (if the width of a river is more than 8m it is shown as two blue lines with a light blue area between). Rivers and streams can be extremely useful in determining your position on a map.

Understanding the shape of the land by looking at a map is a very useful skill and can be essential if you're going to be riding in mountainous terrain. The height and shape of the land is shown on a map using 'contour lines'. These lines appear as thin orange or brown lines with numbers on them – the number tells you the height above sea level of that line. Depending on the map, this may be in either feet or metres – a big difference – so check the map's key to determine this.

A contour line is drawn between points of the same height, so any single contour line will be at the same height all the way along its length. The height difference between separate contour lines is normally 5m, but it will be 10m in very hilly or mountainous areas. The map key will tell you the contour interval used. A few helpful rules to remember about contour lines include:

- Contour lines can never cross one another: each line represents a separate elevation.
- Moving from one contour line to another always indicates a change in elevation.
- The closer contour lines are to one another, the steeper the slope is in the real world.
- Contour lines forming a closed ring shape indicate a summit or ridge.
- Contour lines crossing a stream valley will form a V-shaped pattern pointing in the uphill (and upstream) direction.

Orienting a map

Once you have developed the skills and knowledge to read and understand a map, the next step is to learn how to orientate your map to the land so that you can use it to navigate. One of the best ways to orientate your map is with a compass.

Other uses for a compass

If you are using a compass because you and your ride have had to deviate from your planned route and are not sure exactly where you need to go, it is best to try to find a point that you

Riding Out

recognise and head towards it. Holding your compass flat in your palm in front of your chest, face the landmark. Remember that the red end of the compass points to north, and the black end points to south. Look down at the compass needle to see which way the red point is facing and that will be magnetic north. (Compass readings are affected by the presence of iron and steel objects, so be sure to look out for – and stay away from – pocket knives, belt buckles,

1. **Base plate** – the base of the compass with a ruler for measuring scale.

2. **Compass housing or compass wheel** – this contains the magnetic needle and has the points of the compass printed with a mark every 2 degrees and N, S, E, W.

3. **Orienting lines** – fixed within the compass housing and designed to be aligned with the eastings on a map, on some compasses half the lines are coloured red to indicate north.

4. **The compass needle** – the red end should always point to magnetic north and the white end south.

5. **Orienting arrow** – fixed and aligned to north on the housing.

6. **The direction of travel arrow** – shows the direction that you want to travel along or the bearing you are taking.

7. **Compass scale** – map scales 1:25 000, 1:50 000 and metric measurer.

mobiles and so forth when using your compass.) The angle between the north-pointing needle and the landmark you recognise will tell you the direction you need to head in to reach the landmark – for instance, if the landmark is about 45 degrees to the right (east) of the compass point, it is to the north-east of your current location.

Orientation using land features

As an alternative to using a compass to orientate your map, you can use your eyesight. This method will only work if you are in an area with visible prominent features or landmarks. First, locate yourself next to a feature or landmark and place your finger on the map at the point where you are standing. Then begin to rotate the map so that other features and landmarks on the map begin to line up with the actual ones you can see. The map is now orientated with the land, although not as accurately as it would be using a compass.

When you are planning your route, decide where you want to start from and place your compass on the map. Make sure the 'direction of travel arrow' is pointing in the direction of your route across the map. The easiest way to align the arrow is to place the side of the base plate so it crosses your starting point and the next destination of your journey.

Carefully holding the compass base plate still, you will need to turn the circular compass housing so that the orientating lines on the compass match up with the eastings (the vertical, north-south lines) on your map. Holding the map flat and the compass still, you need to physically turn round so that the compass needle settles in line with the index line.

As you become more comfortable in reading a map you will find that you are able to visualise what the terrain and environment should look like prior to setting off.

GPS systems

The GPS is best-known for its use in cars, where it can tell you exactly how to get to your destination by car, by talking you through it as you travel. Smaller, handheld models are used by hikers, mountain bikers, and there are now several brands on the market aimed specifically at riders. They can tell you how to get where you want to go, show you your track as you make it, and present you with the trail you need to follow.

Unlike a map and compass, a GPS device relies on technology. It receives its information from satellites orbiting the earth. Every 12 hours, each satellite goes around the earth once. As the satellites orbit, they continuously transmit their positions and a time signal. To get the most accurate detail, the GPS needs to connect with at least four of these satellites at once. Most handheld GPS devices are able to pinpoint your location within 15–30m (50–100ft) of accuracy. Accuracy depends on atmospheric conditions, geographical terrains, tunnels, and dense trees. The newer the GPS, the more high-sensitivity the receiver chip, which results in greater accuracy.

Riding Out

When you are using GPS to ride out, the route maps must be stored on the GPS receiver, so the device has a reference for where you're travelling. Most handheld GPS devices come with basic maps loaded already, but if you want to ride on less-travelled routes, you will need to purchase additional maps for the device.

Although different types of GPS devices are available on the market, the best models for trail riders are those designed for hiking and biking. These devices are ergonomically designed, so they're easy to hold in your hand, and can be fastened to your belt or to your saddle. Each GPS is different, depending on the manufacturer and model, but all devices allow you to create waypoints. A waypoint is a spot on your route that you should record for future reference. As you ride along your route, you need to identify places where there is a choice of two or more directions then, the next time you return to ride this route, the waypoints will serve as a guide to help you know where you have been and where you are going.

Whenever using a GPS device, it's a good idea to auto-track your route. Auto-tracking leaves an electronic 'breadcrumb' trail as you ride along, marking the way you have come so, if you want to turn round or if you get lost, the GPS will show you which way to go to get back to your route.

Keep in mind that, because a GPS is an electronic device, it's prone to technical failure. Your battery may die, the terrain may block the satellite signal, or your software may freeze up. For this reason, it's important to also carry an old-fashioned map and a compass as backup. Practically it is a good idea to choose a GPS that has a waterproof case so that it is weatherproof or will survive a water crossing!

You can connect your GPS mapping receiver to your home computer. You can then mark the starting and finishing points on the route maps on your computer, and download them to your GPS. You can select a route, mark it, and put it on your handheld device, so you can follow it when you ride.

Discover Britain on horseback, the official OS mapping app, gives you high-res access to all the OS maps, enabling you to find your local bridleways and plan your routes before you set out. The integrated GPS tracker will help

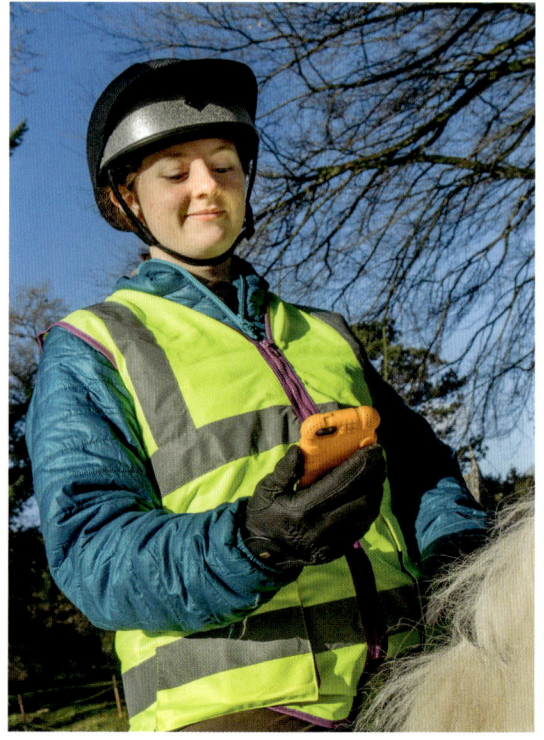

There are GPS apps that can be downloaded onto your smartphone.

you keep track of your current location while you're out and about, so hopefully you'll never get lost. This is particularly useful for long-distance and endurance riders, as well as those who enjoy exploring for fun.

GPS Smartphone App

If purchasing a GPS device is too expensive, you can download applications that use your smartphone's GPS capabilities to help you track your ride. There are many apps available, both free and for a small cost, and a variety of features, such as the ability for you to take photos along the way and post them in real time, along with details of each waypoint, to Facebook or elsewhere online.

Horse Rider SOS

It's every rider's nightmare to fall off and injure themselves while out on a hack, but this app gives peace of mind that, should the worst happen, rescue will soon be on its way. All you have to do is start the app button on your Android or iPhone before you set off on your ride. Nothing will happen so long as your hack proceeds smoothly, but should you fall off your horse, or become unconscious or unable to move, Horse Rider SOS will immediately enter 'Alert Mode' and notify your predetermined guardians that you're in trouble and send your location so that help can be dispatched immediately.

Riding on the road

For the purposes of this section, 'the road' should be understood to mean any route open to vehicular traffic, which includes, for example, byways (*see* Waymarkers, later this chapter) and farm tracks.

While some of the specific requirements of riders by the *Highway Code* are explained in the next section, the following are important general points to remember and practice.

Positioning

When on a road, always make sure you are on the left side. Use your outside (right) leg aids to prevent the horse from swinging his hindquarters into the road. Take a good position at junctions so you can see traffic approaching from any direction and always look, listen and look again before manoeuvring out of a junction. Try to avoid potholes, manhole covers and drains as they can be a tripping hazard, and slippery.

Sometimes on narrow lanes with no verge it may be necessary to move over into a more central position, but always be ready to move out of the way of other road users and be aware of changes in the road conditions and blind bends, which can affect your visibility.

Riding Out

Always try to stay well over to the left when riding on the road.

Signalling

Signalling is a vital skill. It is our way of letting other road (or countryside) users know where we are going, if we intend to turn, or if they need to exercise caution. Make sure all signals or acknowledgements you give to other road users give a driver enough time to react, and are clear and visible. The following are the signals you should be confident in using before you ride out on the road:

Turning left

Your arm must be fully extended at the height of your shoulder, with fingers and thumb close together and the palm of your hand facing forwards. Hold your signal long enough to inform other road users of your planned manoeuvre, repeating it as necessary, depending on the road conditions and behaviour of your horse.

Turning right

This can be more dangerous as you may be turning across another lane of traffic. Extend your right arm fully at the height of your shoulder with fingers and thumb close together and the palm of your hand facing forwards. Again, hold your signal long enough to inform other road users of your planned manoeuvre, repeating it as necessary, depending on the road conditions and behaviour of your horse.

7 | Useful Skills and Knowledge for Planning Rides

Slow down

To ask oncoming traffic to slow down, fully extend your right arm with the palm of your hand facing downwards and move your arm slowly upwards and downwards repeatedly. If you wish to signal to traffic approaching from behind, you will need to turn in the saddle to face it and make the same sign.

Stop

To ask oncoming traffic to stop, use your right arm in the extended position, holding the palm of your hand towards the driver. Again, if you wish to signal to traffic approaching from behind, you will need to turn in the saddle to face it.

Thank you

Many road users will be very considerate so it is important to thank them. You may do this verbally, with a nod of your head and a smile, or by raising your hand if it is safe to do so.

The *Highway Code* rules for horse users

General considerations

- Horses and riders have every right to be on our roads. However, they must follow the Rules of the Road. It is vital that every rider has a clear understanding of the Rules of the Road before taking a horse onto a public road.

- Before riding on the road you should always tell someone where you intend to go and when you will be back.

- If you are riding or leading a horse, you must stay on the left-hand side of the road and obey all Rules of the Road.

- When leading a horse in hand, you should walk so that you are between the horse and the traffic, so as to prevent the horse from interfering with the traffic.

- When riding one horse and leading another one, you must remain on the left-hand side of the road. You should ensure that the led horse is on the left-hand side of the ridden horse, to ensure that you are positioned between the horse being led and the traffic. This is in order to control the led horse, in the interest of safety of all road users. (*See also Highway Code* Rule 53.)

- If you are in charge of a horse on a roadway, you must make sure the horse does not block other traffic or pedestrians.

Riding Out

- It is best not to bring a horse on the road at night. If you do, you should carry a lamp showing a white light to the front and a red light to the rear. You should also wear reflective clothing and put suitable reflective equipment on the horse. (*See also Highway Code* Rule 51.)

- If the weather is bad, you should not ride on the road unless it is absolutely necessary. Motorists will already be experiencing difficult driving conditions and meeting an anxious horse may present a dangerous situation.

If your route takes you on the road in the Republic of Ireland you must be aware of the differences between road signs compared to the rest of the UK.

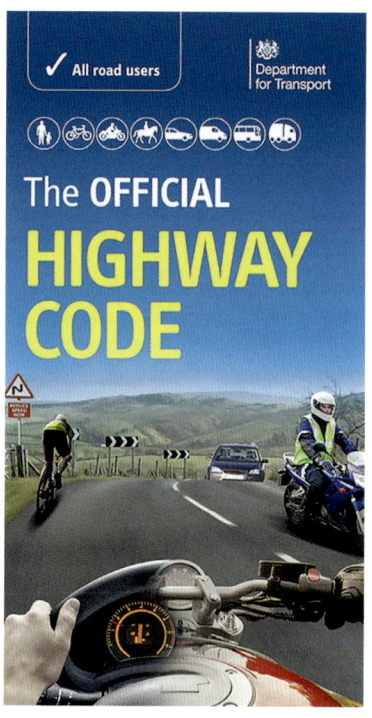

Highway Code booklet.

Specific rules of the *Highway Code* relevant to riders

Some of the points referred to in these rules reinforce or reiterate the general observations made earlier.

Rule 27 Equestrian crossings. These are for horse riders. They have pavement barriers, wider crossing spaces, horse and rider figures in the light panels and either two sets of controls (one higher), or just one higher control panel. (*See also* Rule 54.) There is often a parallel crossing for pedestrians.

Rule 49 Safety equipment. Children under the age of 14 *must* wear a helmet that complies with current hat regulations. It *must* be fastened securely. Other riders should also follow these requirements. These requirements do not apply to a child who is a follower of the Sikh religion while wearing a turban.

Rule 50 Other clothing you should wear.

◊ Boots or shoes with hard soles and heels.

◊ Light-coloured or fluorescent clothing in daylight.

◊ Reflective clothing if you have to ride at night or in poor visibility.

Rule 51 At night. It is safer not to ride on the road at night or in poor visibility but, if you do, make sure you wear reflective clothing and your horse has reflective bands above the fetlock joints. A light that shows white to the front and red to the rear should be fitted, with a band,

7 | Useful Skills and Knowledge for Planning Rides

This photo demonstrates the importance of high visibility clothing – the rider on the left is barely visible.

to your right arm and/or leg/riding boot. If you are leading a horse at night, carry a light in your right hand, showing white to the front and red to the rear, wear reflective clothing, and also fit it to your horse. It is strongly recommended that a fluorescent/reflective tail guard is also worn by your horse.

Rules 52, 53 Safe practice. Before you take a horse on to a road, you should:

◊ Ensure all tack fits well and is in good condition.

◊ Make sure you can control the horse.

◊ Never ride a horse without both a saddle and bridle.

◊ Always ride with other, less nervous horses if you think that your horse will be nervous of traffic.

◊ Before riding off or turning, look behind you to make sure it is safe, then give a clear arm signal.

◊ When riding on the road you should:

111

» Keep to the left.
» Keep a horse you are leading to your left.
» Keep both hands on the reins unless you are signalling.
» Keep both feet in the stirrups.
» Not carry another person.
» Not carry anything that might affect your balance or get tangled up with the reins.
» Move in the direction of the traffic flow in a one-way street.
» Never ride more than two abreast, and ride in single file on narrow or busy roads and when riding round bends.

Rule 54 Road use. You must not take a horse onto a footpath or pavement, and you should not take a horse onto a cycle track. (This is the rule – and, in fact, the law – and it should not lightly be disobeyed. However, in extreme circumstances, it might be necessary to make an exception. For example, if an out-of-control vehicle is hurtling towards your ride, it is clearly sensible to try to avoid it, even if this means mounting the pavement. Similarly, if an emergency vehicle is seeking to pass your ride on a narrow road, it makes sense to step of the way, if safe to do so, long enough to let it pass.)

The equestrian crossings mentioned in Rule 27 should be used as the means of crossing roads wherever possible. You should dismount at level crossings where a 'horse rider dismount' sign is displayed.

Rule 55 Roundabouts. These should be avoided wherever possible. If you use them you should:

◊ Keep to the left and watch out for vehicles crossing your path to leave or join the roundabout.

◊ Signal right when riding across exits to show you are not leaving.

◊ Signal left just before you leave the roundabout.

Basic understanding of the countryside

As a Rider Leader, it is to be hoped that much of your time spent taking rides out will involve riding over terrain that, whether it is a local common or wild upland moorland can, in some sense, can be described as 'countryside'. The following points provide information that will help the successful planning and preparation of rides in the countryside: the next two chapters, which discuss riding out in practice, will deal further with some of these issues.

Categories of land

In order to avoid the possibility of trespass (or even to wander into a potentially dangerous area, such as a military firing range) it is important to understanding whether land is public, private, restricted or has a right of way. In England and Wales access to some areas of land may be permitted at certain times of year, but restricted according to the constraints of the usage of that particular area – for instance, fields with growing crops, and fields containing livestock. Scotland has its own set of regulations which are, in some cases, different from those applicable to England and Wales: these are mentioned separately later in this chapter.

Various methods of research can provide useful information regarding categories of land – in some cases, looking at maps (*see* earlier) may be helpful, as can the BHS guide mentioned in the next section.

Understanding different types of route

When you are riding out in the countryside, you may come across routes marked with different colours known as 'waymarkers'. These take different forms, depending where you live, from paint splashes on trees, to circular plastic discs with arrows. These tell you where you and your horse can and can't legally go. If you are unsure, or keen to find new places to ride, please read the BHS guide at http://www.bhs.org.uk/access-and-bridleways/free-leaflets-and-advice. Below is a snapshot of some of the most common signs and what they mean for you.

- **Footpath.** May be used only by walkers unless you have permission from the landowner – waymarked by a yellow arrow.

- **Bridleway.** May be used on foot or on horseback; horses may be led and in some cases there is the right to drive other animals. Cyclists are also permitted, however they need to give way to horse riders and pedestrians – waymarked by a blue arrow.

- **Byway open to all traffic.** May be used by bridleway users as well as any kind of wheeled vehicle, including motor cars, motorcycles and horse-drawn vehicles – waymarked by a red arrow.

- **Restricted byway.** The same as a byway, except cannot be used by mechanically propelled vehicles such as cars or motorbikes – waymarked by a plum-coloured arrow.

- **Permissive or permitted paths.** Paths for which the landowner has reached an agreement with the local authority to allow linear public access. This permission may be withdrawn or the route altered over time. Permission may be given subject to certain restrictions; it should not be *assumed* that there is horseback access across these routes – waymarked by a white or a black arrow.

Good practice when using these routes

Remember always to keep to the line of a public right of way (or permissive route) unless there is an obstruction (which may include cattle, especially cows with calves – *see the Countryside Code*, later this chapter, and negotiating livestock in the following chapter).

It is likely, even on a designated bridleway/equestrian route, that you will meet non-horse riders such as walkers with dogs, young families with push chairs, cyclists or small motorised mobility scooters. Dog walkers should ensure their dog is under control, and you may need to stop and wait for them to put their dog on a lead before it is safe to pass.

Keep your own speed appropriate to your surroundings and, if possible, keep to one side of the route so that part of the surface is left un-poached for walkers or cyclists. Also be aware that other people may be frightened of horses, so pass them slowly and politely. Whenever possible, acknowledge courtesy shown by other users, especially motor vehicle drivers, to encourage them to keep it up. Please read the BHS leaflet on responsible riding at http://www.bhs.org.uk/access-and-bridleways/free-leaflets-and-advice.

The *Countryside Code*

The *Countryside Code* is a set of rules and guidelines for all users of the countryside, and is intended to protect livestock, property and wildlife for everyone to enjoy for as long as possible. When you are hacking out in the country it's important to respect the countryside

Always pass dog-walkers at walk yourself.

7 | Useful Skills and Knowledge for Planning Rides

and have a good understanding of it. You need to know how the *Countryside Code* specifically applies to you when you are out on horseback – especially when you are responsible for other riders who may not have the same understanding as you. The following sections of the *Countryside Code* explain how adhering to aspects of it will help you, your fellow riders and other users keep safe, and avoid causing nuisance to landowners. As mentioned above, some of the points made by the *Code* are expanded upon in the next chapter, which introduces riding out in practice.

*The **Countryside Code** will help you keep safe and avoid causing nuisance to landowners.*

Fields and gates

Always take care around livestock when crossing fields – animals like cows and other horses can be very inquisitive and potentially dangerous to the horse and rider, especially in the case of mothers protecting their young. Loose horses can find ridden horses coming through their field very exciting and can cause all sorts of problems for your ride. Therefore, always assess a field before entering it, give other animals a wide berth, and keep an eye on the best ways to get out of the field in a hurry if you need to.

If you have reason to open a closed gate, always close it after you. While many gates in the countryside can be operated efficiently by an experienced rider without the need to dismount, be prepared to dismount if you need to in order to ensure that any gate you use is closed and secured in the way you found it. If you pass through an open gate, do not assume it has been left open in error by a previous user (unless you see this happening). Farmers and livestock owners may leave gates open deliberately to allow their animals free access to water or to extend their grazing area, which is why the guideline is to leave gates as you find them, rather than always to shut any gate that you come upon.

Field boundaries, crops and other structures

Do not use other people's hedges, walls or fences as jumps, unless you have the express permission of the owner to do so and have checked for hazards and a safe approach and recovery on both sides. Repetitive schooling on other people's land is not allowed.

If you must pass through a field of crops and it is permitted to do so, stick to the paths or the field margins to avoid damaging it. It's essential to have good control of your horse at all times in fields with crops, as a bolting or uncontrolled horse can easily cause extensive damage.

Do not interfere with any structures such as barns or shelters (this includes matters such as using them as shelter in bad weather). If you notice any damaged structure (including field boundaries) while riding, take what steps you can to alert the owner.

Protecting animals and plants, and avoiding litter

If you see any livestock that appears to be injured or distressed, don't be tempted to try to deal with it yourself but do, if practical, attempt to inform the owner. Similarly, don't interfere with any wildlife you come across on your ride, even if you think it is in distress. Human intervention into the natural lifecycle of wild animals often causes more harm than it prevents.

Don't pick or damage any plants or flowers you come across, stick to paths and bridleways and avoid riding over any 'unspoilt terrain' (e.g. golf courses, etc.) or areas of new plant growth.

Always take your litter home with you, including uneaten food. If you smoke, *never drop cigarette ends anywhere in the countryside* – fire can be devastating to crops, wildlife and property alike, and easily started in the warmer months.

Keep dogs under close control

This section of the *Countryside Code* may not apply to riders specifically, but many riders take their dogs with them when hacking. You should only consider doing this if you know the area well and are confident in your ability to control both dog and horse simultaneously, and are willing and able to dismount if necessary to pick up after your dog. (Even though the *Countryside Code* specifically indicates control of dogs rather than horses, it is only common sense to understand that your horse must also be kept under control at all times, and not cause damage or destruction to wildlife, property or plants.)

Considering other people

Consideration for others is instrumental in getting on in all walks of life, and riding in the countryside is no exception! Hold gates open for other riders if you see them coming, give priority to pedestrians and interact politely with cyclists on any shared paths. If you come across other riders, treat them with respect, make sure you bring your ride back to walk when approaching them, and ask permission to pass them.

Always show consideration to others who are out in the countryside – bring your ride back to walk before passing pedestrians.

Never gallop past walkers or animals or do anything that may cause alarm or inconvenience to other people who are enjoying the countryside too. Keep out of the way of farmers who are actively working with dogs or managing their animals, and do not cause an obstruction by stopping to rest in places that might affect the thoroughfare of a path or walkway. The British countryside is an amazing natural resource – use it safely and with consideration, so that it can be enjoyed by people and animals of all kinds for many years to come.

Regulations and permissions in Scotland

As mentioned earlier, there are some variations between what is or isn't permitted in England and Wales and the situation in Scotland.

In Scotland, those riding and driving horses can now experience a new freedom to access land under the Land Reform (Scotland) Act 2003. This establishes a statutory right of non-motorised responsible access to most land including moorland, forests, farmland and canal banks, and even open spaces in towns. You can find out more about this through the Scottish Outdoor Access Code, but the basic guidelines are as follows. (Note that not *all* of these vary markedly from the position in England and Wales – there are some areas of commonality.)

Land management

In many instances the land on which you will take access will be worked in some way – this means it's someone's livelihood. Do not disrupt ongoing land management, such as ploughing. Access rights do not apply on land in which crops have been sown or are growing, including cereals, vegetables, fruit, and grass being grown for hay or silage where it's at a late stage. You can access field margins or unsown ground, as long as you're careful not to damage the crop.

Paths and tracks

Access on firm, well-drained surfaces and wide paths or tracks causes few problems. On multi-use or shared routes be aware that some people are afraid of horses, so be cheery and polite. If an issue arises dismount if necessary, but give way to walkers, or find an alternative route. Consider the condition of any paths, tracks or fields before accessing them, and on an ongoing basis while you're using them. Please avoid muddy, wet or boggy ground. It's useful to look behind you to make sure you're not causing damage and take an alternative route if horse use is causing erosion.

Farm animals and wildlife

Take care not to alarm farm animals and wildlife. Some animals will act aggressively, so before entering fields check which alternatives are available. Leave gates as you find them, and don't enter fields where there are grazing animals that might be a danger.

Field margins

Field margins are included within access rights, but can be an important wildlife habitat, for example for ground-nesting birds. Land managers may be involved in agri-environment schemes, e.g. protected beetle banks. Take note of any signage including suggested alternative routes, and be aware of ground conditions.

Houses and farmyards

Access rights don't extend to enclosed areas around houses and gardens. In some estates or larger houses, please avoid 'managed policies' (a vague term referring to game bird rearing copses and the like). Respect the privacy of those who live there. Access rights don't extend to farmyards, but if a right of way exists or access has been taken on a customary basis through the farmyard in the past this should continue.

Jumps and schooling

You should get permission before using custom-made gallops, jumps or carrying out repetitive schooling. In some areas, there is and will remain managed access, for instance in some country parks, and you may need to apply for a permit and show insurance. In these cases you should follow local guidance and follow the rules.

Risk-assessing the planned route

Whenever you involve horses there is an element of unpredictability, as even the best-schooled, quietest horse who is as steady as a rock can spook, and the most experienced of riders can fall if caught unawares. Any fall from a horse can result in serious injury. It is also difficult to think of ways to totally minimise the risks in a way that is acceptable to many recreational riders. However, we can take action to reduce the likelihood of an incident occurring and it is in this area that most of the mitigation is done.

As mentioned previously in a broader context, the purposes of a risk assessment are:

- To identify and, where possible, reduce the risk of injury or illness.

- To alert all those taking part of their role and responsibilities in keeping everyone safe.

- In the event of an incident, to provide evidence that risks were identified and that appropriate action was taken to reduce the risks where possible.

The first part of risk-assessing a proposed route is to evaluate the route (a simple sketch layout will be required) and add amendments onto an OS map. If the route is ridden on a constant basis, a standard form may be used, but you need to remember that things do change! You will need to consider crops and animals in fields, route diversions, roadworks and the weather.

One particular aspect to consider in certain areas is the possibility of meeting riders of motorised trail bikes. As mentioned earlier in this chapter, these people are permitted to use byways open to all traffic, so on such routes, this is a possibility to be aware of. If a meeting occurs, the likelihood is that both riders and bikers will be aware of each other in sufficient time for the former to move off the byway (space permitting) and halt, and the latter to slow right down with their vehicles ticking over (or whatever action by both parties permits them to pass safely). However, there are a few areas of actual countryside to which both riders and those practising for trail biking may be permitted access. While the latter, on the whole, are quite considerate of horses, appropriate action on their part is dependent on their being aware of you and, in wooded areas, with engines running, this can't always be guaranteed. If you intend, in principle, to incorporate such areas into the routes of any rides it is useful to talk to local bikers to find out whether there are times when they are more or less likely to use this facility and, if you believe it is likely to be in use on a particular day, to re-plan your ride accordingly.

Further to this perhaps rare example, there should always be room on a generic risk assessment for 'on the day' hazards or concerns and these should be considered carefully prior to setting off.

It is important that those reading the risk assessment document prior to taking a ride out, have a full understanding of what the route is likely to be like – so they can appreciate how the risks have been assessed. Therefore, the centre representative should take care to complete the risk assessment with as much information as possible in order to give a full picture.

EXAMPLE RISK ASSESSMENT FORM

Hazard	At risk	Controls	Action by whom and when
Poor mobile phone signal at any point on the ride.	Impacts on everyone – particularly in the event of an emergency.	Check which service providers have a good signal in the area. Check 999 (112) phone services work at all points on route. Use radio communciations.	Staff and centre representatives to carry walkie-talkies if required.
Poor weather conditions on day of ride.	Riders, centre staff.	Recommend waterproof clothing for all riders. Warm drinks to be carried if a long hack. Facilities to change on return to centre in warm dry area.	Centre staff before, during and after ride.
Boggy ground on route.	Horses, riders.	Prior to ride out, fix hazard tape around the bog. Re-route away from the boggy area. Highlight on map.	Centre staff before and during ride.
Water crossings.	Horses, riders.	Highlight on map and inform riders – alerting rider to river crossing. Check water levels if rain before or during ride and re-route if required.	Centre staff before and during ride.

7 | Useful Skills and Knowledge for Planning Rides

EXAMPLE RISK ASSESSMENT FORM

Hazard	At risk	Controls	Action by whom and when
Busy road crossings.	Horse, rider, other road users.	Check surroundings and suitability of the horses, complete any extra 'on the day' considerations.	Centre staff before and during ride.
Exposed stretches of route.	Horses, riders.	Ride Leader to keep all riders close together and communication throughout.	Centre staff.
Rabbit/badger holes.	Horses, riders.	Mark prior to ride if possible; Leader to display awareness and inform riders.	Centre staff before and during ride.
Low trees.	Horses, riders.	Work with landowner to remove low branches. Warning on map.	Centre staff before and during ride.
Cattle grids.	Horses, riders.	Signs on map; Leader to display awareness and inform riders.	Centre staff before and during ride.
Difficult gates.	Horses, riders.	Ride Leader may need to dismount to open gate.	Centre staff before and during ride.
Slippery surfaces.	Horses, riders.	Ride Leader to give advice as required.	Centre staff before and during ride.
Walkers, bikers or other users.	Horses, riders, other route users.	Warning signs on route to alert other route users.	Centre staff during ride.
Farm animals	Horses, riders, other animals.	Communicate with landowners before ride to request stock be removed from route if likely to cause problems; walk carefully through animals as a group.	Centre staff before and during ride.

Summary

- Go on foot or a bicycle to familiarise yourself with routes before you ride them or speak to your local AROW (Access and Rights of Way) representative.

- Keep abreast of changes in the countryside in your area.

- Read and understand the *Highway Code* and the *Countryside Code* as applicable to horse riders.

Riding Out

- Read the BHS advisory leaflets on riding out.

- Practise hand signals in an arena until you are confident that you can direct your horse with one hand while signalling.

TRAINING TIPS

1. Practise writing a risk assessment of different routes and in varying situations so you can consider how to mitigate risk wherever possible.

2. Keep up to date with local authority websites for any closures of roads or bridlepaths.

3. **RESPECT** the countryside, by memorising and adhering to the following:

   » **R**ide sensibly and always respect others on the roads and paths. It is essential to remember to always give other riders or cyclists enough room when riding past them.

   » **E**veryone deserves respect. Remember to respect others while out and about in the countryside and most importantly always respect farmers. Be sure to leave gates exactly how you found them, or as per the given instructions.

   » **S**tay away from farm machinery and animals. Be sure not to allow the horses in your care to touch other animals, especially other horses, as disease can transmitted this way. Always notify a farmer if you see any animal looking hurt or in danger.

   » **P**rivate means private in England and Wales. Respect people living in the countryside by staying off private property and always abide by no entry signs. Always do your best to stick to designated bridleways and rights of way. In Scotland exercise your right of responsible access only.

   » **E**mbrace the heritage of the countryside but be careful to not disturb historical ruins or sites. It is important to preserve them for future generations to enjoy.

   » **C**onsider the environment at all times. Never drop litter.

   » **T**ake care of the riders for whom you are responsible. You are accountable for your own safety and for the safety of others. Be particularly aware of natural hazards and changes in weather which could lead to extreme conditions.

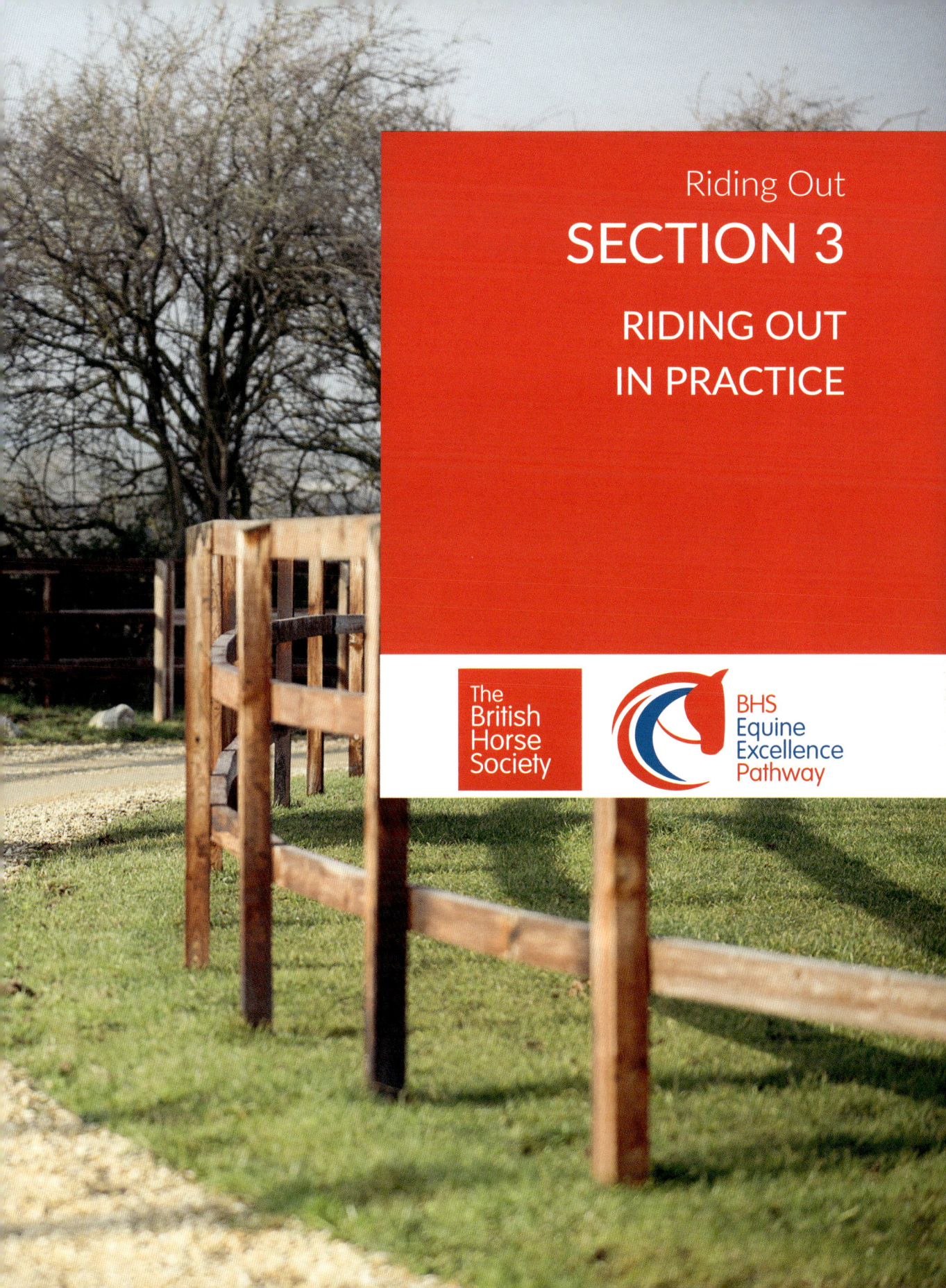

Chapter 8
Leading a Ride Out

Final checks

Ride formation

Negotiating livestock

Opening and closing gates

Basic support and instruction for riders

Injury or illness of a horse en route

Improving riders' skills

Summary

Leading a Ride Out

In this chapter we will look at the key factors involved in leading a ride out, with the general assumption that this will be a ride of relatively short duration (either a 2-hour hack or a 'half-day' ride). Particular considerations required for escorting longer rides (i.e. day rides, or those involving overnight stops in various forms) will be discussed in the next chapter.

Final checks

Plans regarding the actual route and a risk-assessment of it, have already been made but, before leaving the yard, you should ensure that the following points have been attended to.

- A final check for any hazards in the area – road diversions, major bike rides, etc.

- The weather forecast has been checked and conditions are anticipated to be safe for the ride being undertaken. Riders are, in consequence, wearing appropriate clothing (in some conditions, e.g. very cold weather, this might apply to horses, too.) If there are indications that there may be a marked, abrupt change to the weather, you should consider contingency plans. Doing so can have benefits that range from avoiding moderate discomfort to (in severe conditions) avoiding real danger.

Ensure that riders are dressed appropriately for the weather. Warm, waterproof clothing is essential in cold and/or wet weather.

- The riders' clothing is topped by high visibility tabards and horses are wearing high visibility boots.

- A responsible person at the yard has been informed of your route and your estimated time of return.

- You have a fully charged mobile phone that should be capable of receiving a signal in the area of your route. In this phone you should store important numbers of contacts who could help you in an emergency and perhaps an 'ICE' (In Case of Emergency) number so your next of kin can be contacted if you are injured. If possible, the phone should also have an app that allows access to an O/S map of the area, failing which, you should have a hard copy map in your pocket. (In the event that a mobile phone is not available, a walkie-talkie radio may serve, provided that someone at the centre has a similar, connected, device.)

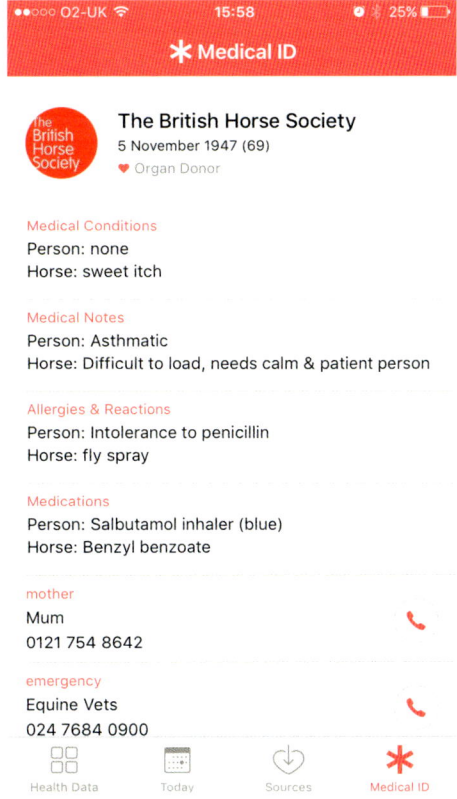

An example of the type of information 'In Case of an Emergency' (ICE) to keep on your phone.

What to take on a short ride out

Other than the items mentioned above, ensure that the following are to hand:

- Lead ropes coiled up and attached to the 'D' ring of each saddle. (These need to coil up carefully so they don't become undone and flap around horse's forelegs.)

- Hoofpick.

- Towelling cloth.

- Fly repellent spray.

- Sunscreen.

- Basic first aid kit for humans and horses.

Riding Out

- Drinking water.
- Energy snacks.

Final checks on riders

The responsibility of a Ride Leader to check tack and equipment has been mentioned earlier (*see* Rider Assessment in Chapter 6), but it is at the point of riding out, certainly for some time and perhaps over testing terrain in uncertain conditions, that it becomes absolutely crucial, so some key points bear repetition here.

- You need to check that the tack is safe for every horse in your ride as you may not be very close to home if problems arise. This may include checking that appropriate bitting is used for any horse who habitually wears a different bit when ridden out than when in the school. It will certainly include last-minute checks to girths – and it is important to remember the need for girths to be checked during the ride, especially before and after any faster work. Particularly with more novice riders, it may be prudent to fit neckstraps to the horses, especially if the ride will include some more challenging terrain. Despite these checks, as a 'belt and braces' measure, it is prudent for you to carry a spare girth, rein and stirrup leather (the latter can be fastened as a neckstrap).

- Tack should be flexible and supple to make sure it is comfortable for the horses and won't cause sores. The stitching, buckles and leather should be in good order so these elements won't break.

- Check that the stirrup bars are in the down position and that the stirrup irons are the right size for the rider's feet. There should be a minimum of 6mm (¼ inch) each side of the foot in the stirrup.

- Another point, useful in the event of a horse getting loose, is to have an identifying tag attached to each saddle, containing information such as the horse's name, name of the centre, and telephone number.

It is vital that the girth is checked and adjusted if required before leaving for the ride.

8 | Leading a Ride Out

Check that the rider's stirrups are level.

- You need to make a final check that everybody's hats are up to standard and their footwear and clothing are safe and appropriate. Long sleeves will offer protection in the event of a fall. Gloves will improve grip on the reins, especially in the wet, and prevent blisters! If riders usually carry a whip, they should take it with them.

While, as Ride Leader, it is your responsibility to check the group's tack and equipment, you should not neglect to do the same for your own. Also, while your riders should be mounted appropriately, so should you. However experienced and capable you may be, it is not appropriate to ride a young, green or unfamiliar horse when you are in charge of a group of riders, as you may have to dismount to help someone, or even lead their horse from yours.

Check that the stirrups are a suitable size for the rider's foot, ideally there should be a minimum of 6mm (¼ inch) each side of the foot in the stirrup.

Riding Out

Observation

When any rider is riding out it is really important that they are aware of the environment and other people at all times. For you, as Ride or Trail Leader, this is even more important, since you have responsibility for your ride and, indeed, should set an example so that they learn to do this themselves. When on the road (or any other shared route) make sure you look all around, listen carefully for other users and assess your surroundings before any manoeuvre or turn. Always make final checks over your right shoulder immediately before carrying out any manoeuvre (including moving off) on the road.

Be aware, also, of any potential shying hazard, so that you can warn riders and prepare them as appropriate. When you look around, try to turn from your waist, and keep both hands on the reins.

Observation and awareness are just as important in the countryside as when on the road, since these qualities can alert you to various potential hazards.

Stay observant of your surroundings at all times; regularly look all around and listen carefully.

Ride formation

When escorting a group, it is advisable that there are no more than eight riders for reasons of safety and practicality. It is always advisable to have a 'back stop' – another responsible rider from the centre who 'rounds up strays' and reports incidents from the rear of the ride, such as approaching traffic, and this becomes essential with larger groups. If you are in charge of a large group on the road, try to ride in double file, leaving between about

Always be aware of any potential hazards that could cause horses to shy.

one horse's length between each pair. If riders usually carry whips, they should do so but, particularly when riding double file, riders should take care that their whip doesn't wave about and irritate a horse alongside them. A sensible way to achieve this is for the inside rider to carry their whip in the left hand, while the outside rider carries theirs in the right hand (the usual hand when riding on a road).

If possible, try to make sure that the horses know each other, or establish whether there are any personality clashes between them and, if there are, try to arrange the group so that such personalities aren't adjacent to each other.

So long as the horses 'get on', riding in pairs on familiar tracks or open ground is also a good plan, since it allows for easy conversation and mutual support between riders.

While you, as Ride Leader, are likely to be at the head of the group this might not inevitably be the case, but in all situations the leading rider and rear rider should be experienced enough to give correct and timely signals to notify other road users of where you intend the group to turn.

Riders leaving the yard.

Where appropriate, riding in pairs can be enjoyable as it allows for easy conversation and mutual support between riders.

Further to this, it is often more sensible for the Ride Leader to be able to have a flexible position in the ride in order to keep an eye on all the group. In this case, if possible, appoint a sensible front rider (perhaps a Ride Helper, or the most experienced rider available), as 'leading file'. When the ride is proceeding one behind the other, leading file has to keep a wary eye out for broken bottles, rusty cans, rabbit holes or boggy ground. The leading file should call out the danger, for example 'beware glass' or 'hole on the left', so that everyone can hear.

One aspect of weather conditions to be aware of is the impact of strong winds on the human voice. Depending on wind direction (and the direction in which the speaker is facing), voice commands given at normal volume may become inaudible. Therefore, in windy conditions, it may be prudent to ensure that all riders remain in fairly close proximity, to give commands more loudly than normal and to check, rather than assume, that riders have got the message. A similar situation can arise simply if there is a large group and the people at the back can't hear – in either case it is sensible to tell riders to pass the message on down the line.

Another role of the leading file is to set the speed of the ride, but this will require common sense and regular observation on the part of that person, so you must remain in overall control of this issue.

It is sensible to tuck the least experienced riders in the middle of the group and, as mentioned earlier, to have another responsible rider for 'rear file'. The rear file warns the others of hazards

It can be useful for the Ride Leader to have a flexible position in the ride so they can keep an eye out for all riders.

from behind, such as overtaking vehicles on roads, and uses hand signals to drivers. The rear file also has responsibility for keeping the ride together so the group doesn't end up being too spread out, so should call out to the leading file to slow down if riders are getting left behind.

The golden rule of riding in a group is that, particularly on the road, you want the ride to be quite close together so that the horses are not too strung out – this is important to avoid the risk of vehicles overtaking part of the group and then cutting in between horses. As Ride Leader, you can help to ensure the cohesion of the group by constantly observing and communicating with the ride and overseeing a speed that is suitable for everyone. Bearing this in mind, you need to plan your route and its timing with the least capable horse and rider in mind.

If cantering in the open, it is still desirable for riders to be quite close together, but you should take care that horses don't get tightly 'upside' each other – which may incite them to race – and that one horse doesn't get too close to the one in front (a point that also applies to riding through water).

Negotiating livestock

It is important to understand that the person who owns land that has a right of way over it may need to use the land to make a living from, and so it should be treated with consideration. The landholder legally has every right to have stock in fields through which rights of way pass, provided that he has assessed that they pose 'no risk' to path users (although, as we shall see, 'no risk' can be hard to establish in absolute terms).

There *are* occasions when it appears that stock are kept in a field, or gates are poorly maintained, deliberately to deter riders. If this is the case, the highway authority has the power and the duty to take action to keep the right of way open and easy to use. Animals making a route hazardous or difficult to pass can be a statutory nuisance under the Environmental Protection Act 1990, and dangerous animals are dealt with by the Animals Act 1971. Should you experience any problems, advice on how to proceed is given later in this section. However, many complaints from path users about stock arise from animal behaviour that is not dangerous, but is perceived as threatening through lack of knowledge and experience, or where the actions of the user have created an unwanted reaction from the animals in the field.

Cattle are naturally very inquisitive.

That said, there have been incidents with tragic results, often without real explanation, because all animals are unpredictable – even experienced farmers handling stock every day have accidents – so you should always be alert. If, as a Ride Leader, you have not had much experience in meeting livestock on rights of way, try to gain experience by riding with someone who is more knowledgeable, and whose horse is accustomed to stock, until you are more confident about what to expect and how to act. This is important when you are responsible for other riders in this type of situation.

Notes on specific animals

Cattle

Cattle are prey animals and not usually aggressive as such, although cows protecting calves, or a bull protecting his cows, do have the capacity for aggression on occasion. However, cattle are notoriously inquisitive creatures, and what may *appear* as aggression is usually just curiosity, especially if they are young, recently turned out onto new pasture, or not handled frequently. Bullocks and heifers may find horses extremely interesting and exciting and a group of young cattle can become very boisterous and 'above themselves' with potentially serious repercussions – especially if one of the horses on a ride becomes 'spooked' by them. (Many horses are impervious to cattle, but a few are really scared of them – a factor to be considered when selecting any such horse for a ride during which cattle might be encountered.)

Longhorn and Highland cattle are often used for conservation grazing and may appear particularly menacing because of their long horns, but they are among the most docile breeds. Dairy cows are handled several times a day and are also of placid breeds, so are least likely to be interested in you.

As with other livestock, passing through fields of cattle calmly will ensure that they get used to horses and quieten down.

Sheep

With reference to the need to pass through stock calmly, be sure never to trot or canter through fields of sheep unless they are far away enough not to be disturbed by you – keep checking, and walk if you are disturbing them. Sheep are most likely to avoid horses and, if they have any concerns, to run from any intruders in their field. However, they could easily be panicked by riders passing near them faster than walk, causing them to run blindly into corners or places where they might be injured. Ewes with lambs are particularly vulnerable, especially on open land. Avoid any action that would cause the sheep to run, as lambs may become separated from their mothers. Also, panic-stricken ewes may abort if they are in lamb.

Be very careful at gates (dealt with later) to ensure that sheep, especially lambs, do not dash through them; this is most likely if they feel cornered or separated from the flock.

Rams can be aggressive and should be treated with caution. They are most likely to be out with ewes during autumn and winter.

Pigs

Many horses are upset by pigs until they become used to them. If your centre is near an outdoor pig farm, contact the farmer to find out if there is any way of familiarising your horses to the pigs in a safe environment before riding through them. Pigs have poor eyesight and are relatively slow-moving, so tend to quickly lose interest in users of a path near them, but they have a strong scent, and this can upset horses even if the pigs are doing very little.

Pigs are increasingly used for conservation grazing purposes to control bracken. They are usually confined by electric fencing, which should not cross the public right of way. This applies on a pig farm too; if the fencing crosses the path it is an obstruction and you may need to involve your highway authority in removing it.

Horses

Loose horses can be the biggest problem when you are riding out. Some horses are naturally more aggressive than most other domestic animals and are more likely to be defensive of their territory.

However, most horses are accustomed to being handled (even 'wild' ponies will be rounded up occasionally) and therefore accept the will of humans. As with cattle, acting confidently but quietly and firmly will achieve best results. Shouting, moving towards them forcefully, waving a whip and acting 'aggressively' will deter most from taking too much interest in you – but be mindful of the effect on your own horse or those of others on the ride!). You may need to turn towards the loose horses repeatedly as you cross the field.

If enough riders cross the field sufficiently frequently, the 'home' horses should become accustomed to the bridleway users and thus less interested. Until they become used to this, it is advisable to have one rider who can deter the loose horses while others negotiate an open gate.

The BHS strongly recommends against stallions being kept in fields through which rights of way pass (*see* BHS Advice on Stallions on Bridleways) but it is not prohibited and does occur in fields and open land. If you are aware of stallions near bridleways and have a mare used on rides out, it is wise to be particularly alert to her being in season and to avoid routes near a stallion at that time. If a stallion is with mares, any strange horse may be at risk, whether male or female.

Other animals

There are many other animals that may be encountered while riding out, whether farmed or not. Bear in mind that, nowadays, the 'farmed' animals may include such as deer, goats, water buffalo, llamas, alpacas, ostriches, emus and geese. Donkeys may also be kept, usually domestically or for breeding. Animals kept for domestic use, or as pets, can sometimes be more of a problem than 'wild' animals, because they have little or no fear of humans and may expect titbits so you may need to be particularly assertive when dealing with them. In general, however, most domesticated animals other than cats and dogs are prey animals and likely to be deterred by confident, calm humans. Nonetheless, all will require greater caution when they have young.

As with animals such as pigs, any problems regarding reaction from the horses on the ride can be overcome by contacting the owner and arranging familiarisation days between the stock and several riders, perhaps starting with just a few stock and increasing their number, if this is feasible.

Increasing safety and avoiding incidents is very much in the interest of the farmer/owner as well as users of the rights of way.

Summary of points to remember

- Any animal that has young may behave differently from normal and should be treated with extra caution as mothers are often abnormally aggressive and highly protective of their babies. What they see as a threat may not be obvious to you.

- Breeding males (such as a bull, ram or stallion) may be aggressive and protective of their females.

- Young cattle and horses in groups may be boisterous, with 'mob mentality'. Be firmly assertive while alert to the situation escalating.

- Animals quickly sense distress and will respond accordingly. Keep calm at all times; be purposeful and quiet in your movements; make your voice strong and confident.

- Frequent riding through livestock usually means the stock react less because visitors are common and no longer interesting. Riding through fields of grazing animals also becomes a familiar occurrence to the visiting horses so they are more likely to react calmly.

There are some important guidelines for riders passing through any livestock:

- Walk quietly through the field.

- Do not ride through any field containing livestock if accompanied a dog.

- Avoid coming between mothers and their young; if your actions may separate them, stop until they are together before continuing slowly.

- If stock are following you closely, turn your horse to face them; they are then more likely to retreat. Shout or move towards them if necessary. You may need to do this repeatedly while crossing the field; keep calm all the time.

- Riders in a group should keep their horses reasonably close together.

Although normally prescribed by the *Countrywide Code*, deviating from the line of a bridleway or byway may be desirable in order to avoid stock (often cattle) lying down. Being off the line of the bridleway is technically trespass, but the cattle are a temporary obstruction on the path and you have a right to deviate far enough to get round them. Since you may not have space to go far enough from the stock to avoid them getting up, approach slowly and calmly, give them time to see you, and they are likely to get up and move away. Use your voice firmly but not aggressively if necessary. If they seem to be scrambling up hurriedly, pause and allow them to calm down before proceeding slowly. Be patient.

If you have had a problem, mention it to the farmer if possible, and see if he has any advice. He is unlikely to be able to move stock from fields with rights of way, but other measures may be possible.

If a problem with livestock is serious and you are not able to contact the owner, or are unable to reach a satisfactory conclusion, your next call should be to your local BHS Access and Bridleways Officer who may know if other riders have been having similar problems and will know the best way to take the matter further in your area. The Officer may be able to resolve the matter with the owner, or will contact the highway authority. You should also inform the highway authority of the problem.

Opening and closing gates

The importance of dealing efficiently with gates has just been mentioned in the context of negotiating livestock and for this, and other reasons, the ability to open and close gates with ease is an important skill for both rider and horse and is a crucial part of the skills of a Ride Leader. The basic training for opening gates mentioned in Chapter 2 will help your horse's responsiveness generally, and being a 'good gate-opener' is a great credit to you and your horse. The following text gives advice on how to do this in practical situations with various types of gate.

Riding Out

The 'heels to hinges' method of operating a gate from horseback

The method recommended by the BHS for greatest safety is commonly called 'heels to hinges' because the horse is positioned facing away from the gate's hinges. It is considered to give riders most control during the manoeuvre and it is most likely to avoid tack being caught by the gate or latch.

To use this method, approach the gate's hinges and turn to position the horse alongside the gate, 'heels to hinges', with the latch by the horse's shoulder and the horse's head and neck extending beyond the latch, parallel to the gate.

The 'heels to hinges' method of opening a gate whilst mounted, the horse is positioned facing away from the gate's hinges.

If the gate opens away from you

With the horse standing parallel to the gate, 'heels to hinges', you lean over to release the latch and push the gate open far enough to give a safe gap. Ask the horse to move backwards far enough to bring his head into the opening, then turn and ride through the gap, bending him around your leg that is nearest the gate. Turn round the end of the gate, push the gate closed and secure the latch. Depending on the space, you may be able to do this positioned either with the horse's head or heels to hinges.

If the gate opens towards you

With the horse standing parallel to the gate, 'heels to hinges', lean over and open the latch, then move the horse sideways away from the gate while keeping one hand on the gate and drawing it with you. Move forwards and turn round the end of the gate when the opening is wide enough.

Once through the gateway, you may be able to move your hand along the gate towards the hinges, drawing the gate closed, then backing to secure the latch, or you may need to turn the horse 'heels to hinges' parallel to the gate and then move sideways while drawing the gate closed.

Best practice

Best practice is to keep a hand on the gate at all times to give greatest control over it. If the gate is pushed wide, or taken wide by its weight, or the wind, then it takes much longer to ride after it and to close it, so stock are more likely to escape. The uncontrolled swing could damage the gate and, if the gate swings closed, it could hit the horse or rider's leg.

However, many riders, especially with large horses, cannot keep hold of the gate. In this case, extra care is required, particularly where stock are present and the rider must be ready to prevent the gate swinging wide or closed, only pushing or pulling the gate as hard as necessary to create a safe gap – it should never be flung wide.

Self-closing gates

Letting go of the gate to ride through the gap is not safe with gates that close quickly, as the closing gap may cause the horse to panic, or horse or rider may be hit by the gate or the post. If the gate closes itself, you need to keep one hand on the gate to hold it open or push it again until your horse is clear. Always check that it has secured before riding away. Check the closing speed of unfamiliar gates before letting your horse enter the gap, as some get faster as they close and a gate closing on a horse is very dangerous. If you cannot reach to hold the gate open, you may be safer to dismount.

Two-way opening gates give riders a choice of opening the gate towards or away from them. It is commonly assumed that, given that option, riders will always open a gate away from them, but some riders find that they have more control moving the gate towards them – for example, if a horse tends to rush through a gap opening in front of him.

Where the 'heels to hinges' method can't be used

It may not be possible to use this method if there is no space for the horse's head and neck beyond the latch, or if there is not enough space to come alongside the gate.

Riding Out

Many horses and riders manage to negotiate gates with the horse's head over the gate, but it is less safe because riders will often need to swap hands, potentially losing control; there is greater risk of the reins or martingale being caught; and the gate or latch may hit the horse's head. Much depends on the latching mechanism – a latch that has to be held open while the gate clears it is more difficult to open when not parallel to the gate. Self-closing gates with a fast speed can be impossible to operate with this method, or take several attempts, which can be tedious, time-consuming and increase the risk of injury, so it is best practice to dismount to deal with these.

With such gates (or any others where it is necessary to hold the gate open for other riders to go through), make sure you do not put your own horse in a position where he may get trapped or kicked by another. Inform your riders to put the reins in one hand and keep the hand nearest the gate free to catch it if you should inadvertently let it go.

Opening a gate to allow other riders to go through.

Basic support and instruction for riders

As mentioned earlier, many people choose to ride outdoors basically to enjoy being in the open air while riding a horse. Although such riders have not signed up for a riding lesson in an arena, there are occasions when providing instruction and guidance allows them to enjoy their riding experience more thoroughly.

It is important for the Ride Leader to interact with the riders at all times and to provide a level of instruction that keeps riders safe and enables them to enjoy their riding.

Clues to what might be necessary or helpful may have been noticeable during the pre-ride assessment, but points requiring attention will be more evident to the Ride Leader who remains observant and is prepared to maintain a dialogue with the riders. This approach should, in fact, begin before the ride starts. When allocating horses and assessing riders, the Ride Leader should ensure that riders are both physically and mentally comfortable and should try to maintain a conversation with them, even if this is just the occasional explanation of what is happening, and why. This makes riders feel more involved, signals that the Ride Leader is happy to interact with them, and makes it more likely that they will be happy to ask questions or express concerns.

The Ride Leader should regularly check all riders and provide instruction as required to keep riders safe and ensure the ride is enjoyable.

Riding in walk

When riding in open country, the rider's position in walk should be relaxed, with the horses also walking in a relaxed manner, but you should be prudent in your observation of, and advice to, riders, especially if they are quite novice. For many novice riders, the concept of maintaining a light rein contact is one they find difficult. At one end of the spectrum, they may have little or no discernible contact; at the other end of the spectrum there may be an unnecessarily tight hold on the reins. In the interests of both riders and horses, it may be prudent to explain (without nagging) the desirability of a light but fairly consistent contact on a reasonable length of rein. More experienced riders will be able to exercise judgement as to when it is appropriate to let horses go on a truly long rein, with no actual contact but, unless circumstances clearly indicate that it is safe to do so, it is not advisable to encourage true novices to ride with no contact, because this gives horses the opportunity to try to snatch mouthfuls to eat, which could either unbalance the rider or result in a horse ingesting something harmful and also, if something startles the horse, he will immediately be out of control, since few novices will be able to gather up the reins fast enough to prevent it.

Riding in trot

When riding out, trot work should normally be ridden rising – the one possible exception perhaps being when riding past a potential shying hazard. For novices, rising trot should be used pretty much all the time, because it is unlikely they will be able to sit to trot over open terrain.

Before moving into trot, assess the terrain and check that all the riders are in control and likely to maintain safe distances between each other. Inform riders how long the trot is likely to be, choosing in your mind at what point you will return the ride to walk. Avoid long periods in trot, particularly if the riders are unfit or inexperienced. Likewise, avoid moving downhill in trot (or canter) unless riders and horses are both fit and experienced. Trot and canter (if applicable) on a flat piece of ground or uphill. Whenever possible try not trot and canter, start and stop, in the same place on every ride out.

Leading a rider

If, when you are leading a ride, a rider becomes anxious, it may be necessary to lead them from your horse until they feel more confident. Therefore, as mentioned at the start of this chapter, a lead rope of reasonable length should always be carried when riding out so that, if a rider is struggling to control a horse, or they are becoming nervous, then ride and lead is an option.

In order to make sure that you (and the horses) are confident with this procedure it is worth practising this at home in an enclosed space, as mentioned in Chapter 2. This will also minimise the chance that your horse, and the one to be led, have an aversion to each other. (In the unfortunate event that they do, it may be necessary to resort to some horse swapping with another rider who has no personal concerns.) The horse being led should always be on the left-hand side of your ridden horse.

Procedure on a ride out

First, reassure your nervous rider that they are safe and you are going to help them.

If a rider becomes anxious whilst out on a ride it may be necessary to lead them from your horse until they feel more confident.

To ride and lead safely, you first need to halt all of your riders in a space that is big enough to maintain a safe distance between them and where they will not cause a hazard to anyone else. When doing this as a group on a hack try to divide into groups of two before you halt – i.e. allow spaces between each pair of horses.

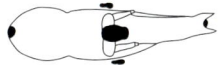 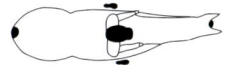    

Turn your horse and the horse you are going to lead at a 90-degree angle to each other. Dismount to clip the lead rope on and pass it through the offside (right) bit ring and clip it to the nearside (left). You will be leading the rider from your left.

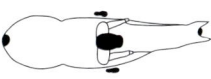 

Riding Out

Whilst mounting, position your horse at 90 degrees to the horse you are going to lead.

Remount your horse, paying attention to both horses. Ideally, ask a helper to lead the second horse alongside your knee to start with until you are all comfortable with this positioning, before taking the lead rope yourself. However, if this is impractical, you will have to start leading from the moment you remount. Keeping the led rider informed at all times as to your movements, walk gently forward, telling your led rider how to keep their horse alongside the shoulder of your horse.

If you have to go along the road in this situation, it is appropriate to nod and smile at drivers who slow down rather than taking one of your hands off the reins. Remember that you will need to talk to your led rider to explain when you may be going to speed up or slow down. If you are on a road, you should consider how wide it is, as narrow roads may not be wide enough to let traffic pass two horses side by side. In this situation, make sure that the led horse will follow quietly behind your horse, but not so close that he steps on the heels of your horse. The same procedure may be necessary if you are on a track or path that is very narrow.

When leading, you should go no faster than trot to avoid excitement. It is important to make sure that the horse being led can comfortably keep up with the speed of the horse you are riding.

Dealing with falls

Accidents can be minimised by correct preparation and safety checks before leaving the yard, and by exercising sound judgement and awareness in your role as Ride Leader. Further to this, the most common causes of more serious accidents as a result of a fall when riding out are:

- People leading rides who lack knowledge and attention to detail (which is why qualified Ride/Trail Leaders are to be preferred).

- Failure to match horse and rider.

- Going too fast on dangerous terrain.

- Failure to check the tightness of the girth a first time and a second time after a few minutes of riding.

- Improper mounting and dismounting.

- Riding when rider is unfit or unwell.

- A hat or coat falling from a horse in front and spooking the ones behind.

- A kick from another horse.

- Rider getting left behind and the horse speeding up to catch up.

- Having too many riders for the number of guides/escorts.

- Tired horses and riders.

It will be evident from this list that many falls may be avoidable if due care is taken. However, despite this, it remains a fact that falls can happen at any time and it's important to know what to do in that situation.

Before you take rides out, you will need to take a first aid course (a requirement of the Ride/Trail Leader qualifications). This will prepare you for all sorts of emergencies and give you the confidence and skill to handle things like fractures, concussions and other injuries that can happen when riding or handling horses.

If a rider and their horse do 'part company' you will have to take a quick assessment of the situation.

Sometimes riders will hold onto their reins, dust themselves down, and remount. Even if they seem fine, you should still check this with them verbally. If they seem just a little shaken, it is prudent to tell them to take a few moments to recover their composure and to dismount yourself, steadying their horse and giving assistance as they remount. However, if any 'shakiness' includes their turning pale, sweating or trembling, you should be prepared for the eventuality that there might be a significant problem, at which point you should make further enquiries and not be in a hurry to help them remount unless or until they appear to have recovered within a few minutes.

In the case of a really bad fall, you will have to look after the rider as a priority, even if the horse leaves the scene.

If the rider needs first aid or medical attention, this may be the time when carrying a fully charged mobile phone can be a huge help, so long as you know that there will be a compatible signal available on your route. This can also be the time when the advantages of following a pre-arranged route becomes apparent, as well as letting someone know where you are going and your estimated time of return.

Only once the rider has been looked after is it time to look to the horse. If the horse has left the scene, and you are on familiar territory, he will probably find his way home. If not, he may seek companionship and safety near other horses, or even other livestock. If the horse isn't found quickly, contact the yard so that they can mobilise help to search for him and notify the appropriate authorities, providing clear photos and a description. (The 'appropriate authorities' will depend partly on the circumstances – for example, if the incident happened on or near a road, this will be the police; if in a park or enclosed areas such as NT land, park rangers or similar personnel.) Begin your search at the place the horse was last seen. Notify anyone living in the vicinity and leave your contact information with them. If there is a competent back-up escort available, they might be dispatched to look for the loose horse.

Injury or illness of a horse en route

If horses are known to be fit and healthy before setting out on a ride, and due care is taken by both the Ride Leader(s) and clients, the chances of problems arising during the ride will be minimised. However, that is not to say that they can be eradicated – even a well-balanced horse may slip on a patch of false ground, or step on a half-buried root or rock, and a novice rider, in a moment of inattention, may allow their horse to snatch a mouthful of a poisonous plant.

There are many illnesses and injuries that horses can suffer from, and Ride Leaders are not expected to have the skills of a vet, but being aware of the most common issues and how to deal with them, at least in principle, is essential for anyone leading rides out. This can be supplemented by a working knowledge of basic equine anatomy, which can be useful in the event of any emergency phone conversations with a vet, and can inform your assessment of certain injuries – for example, an apparently small (but penetrating) wound over a joint can quickly lead to a severe infection which, if left untreated, can prove fatal.

Many equine veterinary practices offer training classes in equine first aid you may find it useful to attend such sessions.

Assessing lameness

If one of the horses in your care suddenly goes lame, you should ask the rider to dismount immediately. Pick up the lame leg and check that there isn't a stone or other object such as a nail in the hoof. If there is nothing sharp in the hoof and the horse can put weight on the injured leg and you can identify that there is a farm or yard nearby, lead him slowly there to get help. However, if there is a sharp object such as a nail or piece of metal in the hoof, telephone the vet immediately. Depending on the area of the foot that has been penetrated and how far you are from a farm or yard, the vet will advise you as to whether removing the object is recommended and, if so, how best to do this. If the object needs to be removed immediately to prevent further damage, take photographs of it in situ first so that you can show the vet when they arrive. It is vital that the nature of the hoof penetration is known by the vet to allow them to give the most appropriate treatment.

If there is nothing visible in the foot and the horse is reluctant to weight bear on that leg, do not try to move him and seek professional help in situ from a vet.

Removing a shoe

If the problem is a loose or twisted shoe, you may have to remove the shoe yourself. If it is a front shoe, pick up the horse's leg and place the foot between your legs just above your knees. If it is a hind shoe, lift the leg and rest it on the tops of your legs, above the knees. If you have suitable tools to knock up the clenches, it may then be possible to remove them one by one, but sadly it is not usually this easy! Using pincers or another suitable tool to act in lieu (wire cutters or similar), start at the back of the heel on one side and pull inwards to lift the shoe off the heel. Swap to the other side and lever that side loose. Work your way forward to the toe and try to pull the shoe off in a straight line in order to limit the damage to the hoof.

Minor injuries

Any superficial scrapes or grazes should be thoroughly cleaned with copious amounts of an appropriate antibacterial solution such as dilute chlorhexidine (Hibiscrub®).

Sterile wound gel can then be applied using clean gloves. It is important not to contaminate the wound any further by applying gels or creams with dirty hands. Deeper wounds should initially also be treated in this way to reduce contamination by dirt and bacteria as soon as possible, before being treated by a vet. If a wound is bleeding, apply firm pressure for at least

10 minutes using a clean cloth. If the bleeding has not stopped after 10 minutes, continue to apply firm pressure until the bleeding does cease. Telephone the vet and, provided the horse is able to walk, lead him to the nearest yard or farm where further treatment can be carried out.

Colic

If a horse shows any signs of colic, he should be dismounted immediately and, provided it is safe to do so, the saddle should be removed to avoid the horse injuring himself if he rolls. Be aware that horses in severe pain are dangerous as they can roll or kick out violently and unpredictably. If it's safe, lead the horse for several minutes to see if the signs subside. Telephone the vet, who will discuss the signs and decide whether the horse should be assessed. Remember that all colic is potentially life-threatening so it is vital to get prompt professional advice, even if the signs seem relatively mild or subside quickly. If colic occurs on a ride out, inform the vet if there's any suspicion that the horse may have ingested some harmful plant.

Serious injury

If the horse is seriously injured in any other way you may have to go for help (or send someone competent). It is important not to leave the injured horse alone, as he may panic.

If you have to phone for help, and cannot for some reason make contact with your usual vet, the British Equine Veterinary Association (BEVA) keeps an up-to-date list of practices that have been specially trained in large animal rescue in conjunction with the emergency services. This list can be found on their website and the section covering your area is worth taking with you as a back up when you ride off the beaten track.

Improving riders' skills

If riders basically enjoy the experience of riding out, it is likely that many of them will want to improve their skills, broaden their experience and, in due course under progressive guidance, learn to take on new challenges. More experienced clients will be expecting to confront most of the challenges in this section as a matter of course, but they might still benefit from occasional tips.

Riding up and down hills

The ideal when riding up and down hill is that the rider should adapt their posture to maintain dynamic balance with the horse, but this can be quite difficult to explain to novice riders, and advice is best offered in simple, general terms.

When riding uphill, the rider's upper body should be inclined forwards, and it is best to explain this using terms such as 'incline' or 'fold from the hips' because, if riders are told to 'lean forwards', they may pivot at the seat, so their legs swing back behind the girth (reducing the effectiveness of leg aids) and they tip onto their fork, reducing security. They should also be told that the horse is likely to want to stretch and lower his head and neck and that they should allow their hands (and thus the reins) forward to let him do so.

Tell your riders to steady their horses before starting to ride downhill, and to try to maintain steady progress. When riding downhill, it may be necessary (and will feel safer for novice riders) to sit back a little, and they can be advised to do this but again, an unqualified instruction to 'lean back' should be avoided, because misinterpretation and/or exaggeration may be unhelpful to both horse and rider. If the rider leans right back on the cantle, this will overburden the horse's hindquarters when he needs to engage them to retain balance; if the rider does this without lengthening the reins/reducing the contact, the horse will tend to hollow, compromising his balance even further. Also, if the rider's exaggerated leaning back involves pivoting at the seat, their legs will swing too far forwards to be much use when giving aids. (Although they may not want to give aids to ask for more forward movement, it is important that the legs are available to help the horse keep moving straight – an important aspect of riding downhill that should be mentioned to all riders.)

Riders will need to adapt their position when riding up and down hills in order to remain in balance, and may need other advice as to how to negotiate hills.

Riding through water

When moving through water, riders should walk, trying to keep their horses moving and maintaining a safe distance (a couple of lengths) between each. If a horse is reluctant to move through water it should not be down to the client rider to tell the horse what to do, hence the need of ensuring that horses have already been acclimatised to water (*see* Chapter 5).

When riding through water riders should keep their horses moving and maintain a safe distance from the horse in front.

Riding over difficult terrain

It would not be prudent to take novice riders over significant areas of difficult terrain. However, there may be occasions when tackling a short section of rough terrain is expedient in terms of the whole ride, and other occasions when ground conditions change suddenly. More experienced riders may choose to visit areas where the terrain in general is quite wild so, one way or another, a Ride Leader should be prepared to tackle difficult terrain, exercising due prudence and giving the ride appropriate

Make riders aware of terrain change. For example, you may need to provide advice as to how they negotiate particularly stony ground.

advice. One point to consider is the fact that surface changes may affect the speed of the ride. For example, normally good going can become slippery when wet; heavy rainfall can turn tracks from slightly muddy to really deep and 'holding', while hot sunshine on the latter can turn it into something similar to cobbles.

Riders will always feel more confident if they are made aware of changes of terrain. For example, if you are moving the ride downhill over some stony going, you should encourage the riders to allow their reins to be a little longer (while maintaining a light contact) and to sit slightly back in order that horses can maintain balance and be sure of foot.

Riding at faster gaits

If you know that you are going out for a hack with more experienced clients that will include some faster work, it is a good idea to adjust stirrup leathers in a way that would suit all terrains and circumstances. This is likely to be shorter than they would expect to ride if they were having a flat riding lesson in the school, but longer than if they were working over fences. The length of leathers should be short enough to support them in a forward seat but not so short as to be uncomfortable over a long period.

The forward seat is often referred to as 'jumping position', to which it is similar and you may, at times, instruct riders to take a forward seat if, for example, you are intending to canter or gallop.

The forward seat is quite simple; tell the riders to fold their upper body forward while, at the same time, lifting their seat from the saddle and holding their weight balanced on their legs.

A rider cantering in forward position.

Riding Out

When in the forward seat, tell riders to keep their hips balanced in line with their heels. Bear in mind that this can be quite tiring for riders who are not using to working in this position. Therefore start off with relatively short spells. (If riders are using Western tack, riding in the faster gaits will need to be in a posture appropriate to that style, which precludes the forward seat as just described. Further to this, jumping is Western tack is difficult and best avoided.)

Horses are creatures of habit with good memory. They will remember which parts of the hack are faster than others and may anticipate this and become 'strong', thinking they are going to canter or gallop. Therefore, when possible, try to keep this faster part of the ride working uphill. Also, although it can be difficult to manage in some areas, try to vary routes whenever possible and avoid always cantering or galloping in the same place.

There is nothing wrong with putting in some gallop work when out hacking, however it is just as important to school horses in order that they are not only willing to go forward and work faster but also willing to slow down when asked. This may take some time and may require work by experienced riders.

Ensure that all riders are provided with the basics of how to control the horse in any eventuality. Riders will only gain confidence to move faster over time. When possible this should be developed through the canter work. Selecting horses is important, knowing that a rider's first experience of going faster is important and influential, and is developed over successive rides when opportunities arise. It is, of course, important that you tell riders how to slow down and that the horses are willing to oblige, but it is equally important to explain how to move into the faster gaits smoothly and under control because, if control is established at the outset, it is much easier to retain it. Riders who progressively gain the confidence to steady their horses down in canter will slowly develop the confidence to gallop. We all start with a poor understanding and feel for speed: we think we are going fast when often we are not in much more than a canter.

Bridging the reins

When clients start riding at the faster gaits in the open, it is worth telling them how to bridge the reins. This technique, used widely in racing, helps to ensure an even contact on both reins (desirable unless a rider is employing the 'emergency stop' technique described above). To form a double bridge, the top of each rein is taken over the rein in the opposite hand.

Bridging the reins allows the rider to hold the bridged rein in both hands which helps to keen an even contact and can be used in faster paces.

If a rider loses control at speed

Despite taking all reasonable precautions regarding where and when to you allow the ride to go faster, and giving appropriate instructions about how to proceed, the unfortunate position may arise of a horse working too fast, with the rider feeling as if they are being run away with. In such a situation, stay behind the horse in question in order that a racing situation is not created. Call to the rider to keep their weight on their legs, to try not to grip up with their legs, to come more back from their forward position and pull back on one rein while keeping the other rein held steady. If you are on a straight path, then a straight line ahead is the only option, but in a more open space on good ground, telling the rider to circle away is often the best course of action.

Summary

- Make sure that you are fully prepared before you leave the yard and that you have informed someone of your route and planned return time.

- For all riders, check:

    » They are wearing high visibility clothing.
    » Hats are correctly fitted, fastened and up to date.
    » All riders are wearing suitable clothing and footwear.
    » All riders are correctly mounted and in control of their horses.

- For all horses, check:

    » The horse is wearing high visibility boots.
    » Tack is correctly fitted and safe.
    » Shoes/feet are in good condition.

- Give clear instructions before any change of gait, speed or terrain.

- Make sure that nervous riders are close to you and that the horses have sufficient space between each other.

TRAINING TIPS

1. Practise mounting and dismounting safely from the ground and from a mounting block.

2. Make sure that you know how to prepare yourself and all the horses in your care prior to any hack out.

3. Spend some time riding all the horses out that you sensibly can, on frequently used routes so that you know that they will cope with any eventualities you may come across.

4. Practise hand signals in an arena until you are confident that you can direct your horse with one hand while signalling.

5. Practise how to manage in an emergency in a variety of situations.

Chapter 9

Planning and Leading Longer Rides

Notes on planning

Managing breaks and overnight stops

Summary

Planning and Leading Longer Rides

Although many riders who sign up for longer/more arduous rides are likely to be reasonably experienced, that cannot be *assumed*. Therefore, all the points made in the previous chapter regarding assessing and supporting riders must be adhered to when preparing for and escorting longer rides. Risk-assessing routes for longer rides, and general planning, must be done very thoroughly – the latter may include pre-booking of accommodation for both horses and riders in the case of rides that include overnight stops.

While these longer rides should be supervised by a Stage 3 Trail Leader, Stage 2 Ride Leaders may act in supporting roles.

Notes on planning

Most long rides in the UK are carefully pre-planned for good reasons. The following are some points to consider.

Routes and timing

Safe routes for long rides are not mapped in all locations, and those that do exist may not go where you want. The BHS is the chief national promoter of routes and information can be found at bhs.org.uk/access and bridleways.

Assuming that various routes have been tried and tested by staff previously, decide how long you intend your ride to be away from the yard and choose on your route accordingly. Consider that your daily mileage may vary, depending on the terrain, weather, availability of water and grazing, etc. It is also important to decide how long the riders are able to spend in the saddle each day and to plan how early you are going to start every morning. (When calculating starting/finishing times, remember to take account of seasonal variations in daylight.) The distances covered will also make demands of the horses, so it should go without saying that those used should be suitably fit and well shod. A horse or pony on an average hack travels at about 9km (5½ miles) an hour so, factoring in occasional stops, a 33km (20 mile) ride would take some 4 hours.

If you are planning to be out all day you will have to build in about an hour for lunch, and a bit more for rest breaks on the way.

Accommodation

Depending on the ride envisaged, this may range from a lunchtime stop at a picnic area or pub, through to a campsite or B&B or 'horse hotel' accommodation. All will require an element of pre-planning.

Picnic areas (even if on open ground) may need to ensure that they are safe for horses (free from poisonous plants, litter, etc.) and, perhaps, suitable for sharing with members of the public.

Pubs may require meals for parties to be pre-booked, and certainly consulted to check that they have a secure area to accommodate the horses.

If camping on open ground is envisaged, then checks need to be made to ensure that this is permitted, the area will need to be reconnoitred to ensure that it is safe and suitable for people and horses. Consideration will need to be given to human factors such as type and provision of tents and toilet facilities and how they are to be provided. Regarding the horses, security and the provision of food and water are paramount.

If the intention is to use a commercial campsite, this may require pre-booking. Other than the fact that such a site should have lavatory facilities for the riders, the same issues as for camping on open ground need to be addressed.

B&B or hotel accommodation for riders, along with suitable accommodation for horses, will definitely need to be booked in advance.

Before undertaking any long ride that includes overnight stays, visit the facilities you have identified to accommodate the horses. You will need to consider factors such as the proximity of the human accommodation to the horse's as it is unlikely that you will have any other form of transport. There should always be water available for the horses, and also shelter, especially in exposed areas or in case of inclement weather. The boundaries need to be secure and you may need to consider, when choosing horses for the ride, whether they will socialise together when you turn them out as a herd.

If any pre-booking of accommodation is involved, this may also involve pre-payment of deposits, at least. It is important to be aware of any costs additional to those of the actual ride (i.e. the hire cost of the horse) and to make these known to clients in advance of the ride.

Equipment and provisions for a long ride

For supporting riders

- *Maps.* Make sure that you have detailed maps (whether hard copy or available through phone apps) of all the areas you wish to ride through.

- *Compass.*

- *Fully charged mobile phone.* It is useful to investigate the strength of the signal in the areas you will be travelling beforehand so that you are prepared! It is also a good idea to take a power bank for extra charge and charging cables just in case you stay somewhere there is power available.

- *Wrist watch.*

- *Whistle.* Use it to sound for help or signal a warning; the piercing sound carries further than a shout, and takes a lot less wind. The international distress signal for a whistle is six loud blasts repeated at 1-minute intervals.

- *Flashlight* with charged battery.

- *Suitable clothing.* There's an unwritten rule about whether to take rain gear on a ride: if you have it, the sun will shine; if you don't have it, it'll rain! A storm can blow in when you least expect it, especially in exposed places, and few things will leave people more miserable than being soaked to the skin with miles still to ride.

- *Food.* It is really important to have some sort of energy source with you, as you never know when a rider may need a blood sugar infusion or your ride may take longer than you have planned! It is a good idea to choose non-bulky foods suitable for carrying on horseback, such as energy bars, nuts, cubed melon and sliced or dried fruit. These are easy to grab and eat while walking on horseback. Sandwiches, however, tend to fall apart if you have one hand on the reins while you try to eat. Sports drinks bridge the gap between being an energy source and a form of hydration.

- *Water.* Even if you don't get thirsty enough to drink it, you never know when you might need water for cooling down an overheated horse or rider, or for rinsing out a wound. It is important to ensure that riders remain hydrated. (This also applies to horses, but general provision for watering them is dealt with separately, in the next main section of this chapter.)

- *First aid items.* Your list of items can be as simple or detailed as you wish, but it is good practice to keep all first aid items in a single bag, and colour-code it for easy recognition during an

A first aid kit can be carried in a bum bag; it is then easily accessible in an emergency.

emergency. Choose a red bag, for instance, or tie a red ribbon round the box or bag. (Some basic first aid items for horses should also be carried.)

- *Toilet paper*. At least one roll may be expedient for a half-day ride. If overnight camping stops are involved, it may be sensible to take more.

For supporting horses

- *Headcollars and lead ropes* for all horses. (Headcollars may be fitted under bridles.)

- *Lunge rein* for grazing in hand.

- *Baling twine.* Sufficient baling twine to be split into strands to tie up all horses, if necessary.

- *Hay*, or other fodder, for as many days as you will be staying.

- *Feed* (if you'll be there for 'mealtimes'). Provision of feed and hay for stops on long rides should be organised in advance, and is likely to have been supplied or delivered separately from the ride itself.

- *Electrolytes*.

- *Hoofpick*.

- *Hoof boot*. Can be used as a 'spare tyre' for lost shoes or for horses or ponies who are barefoot and the terrain is likely to be stony or hard.

- *Duct tape*. This has many uses, from mending tack to protecting a hoof when a shoe has been lost.

- *Stethoscope* (to check pulse/respiration if a horse seems distressed).

- *Plastic shopping bags.* Weighing almost nothing, these have lots of uses. Examples: slip one over each boot to keep them dry during a cloudburst; create a makeshift water carrier; make a compress holder or bandage cover.

- *Sharp knife or folding multi-tool.* This can be used to free a rope-entangled horse or to pick out a horse's feet, or even to cut open your provisions if required. It is a good idea to carry it securely on your person rather than putting it into a bag carried on your horse so that you can access it instantly should an emergency occur.

Riding Out

Managing breaks and overnight stops

Feeding and watering horses

As a general rule it is a good idea to allow about 15 minutes grazing time every for 1½hours (with the bit removed assuming that the horses are wearing headcollars under their bridles), but you will need to be sensible and pick opportunities where there is suitable grazing. At lunchtime, it is ideal to untack the horses and allow them to roll if they wish – although this is not such a good idea if it is pouring with rain, in which case at least bridles should be removed, and girths loosened. If possible, the bits should be washed off before the bridles are replaced.

Depending on the accommodation for the horses on an overnight stop, you may need to feed concentrates, but they should all have ad lib fodder (grass or hay) at this point.

It is really important to ensure that horses do not become dehydrated. If, on the ride, you pass fresh running water that you are confident is not contaminated, then encourage the horses to drink wherever possible. If you have any concerns and wish to test for dehydration, pinch the skin on the horse's neck. It should return back to being flat and smooth immediately. If he is dehydrated it will take longer than 2 seconds to return to normal. As mentioned earlier, you should pre-check that anywhere intended as an overnight stop should have fresh water available, and make such arrangements as necessary to ensure that horses have access to it. (For example a campsite may well have a water tap, but you might need to arrange a supply of buckets from which the horses can drink.)

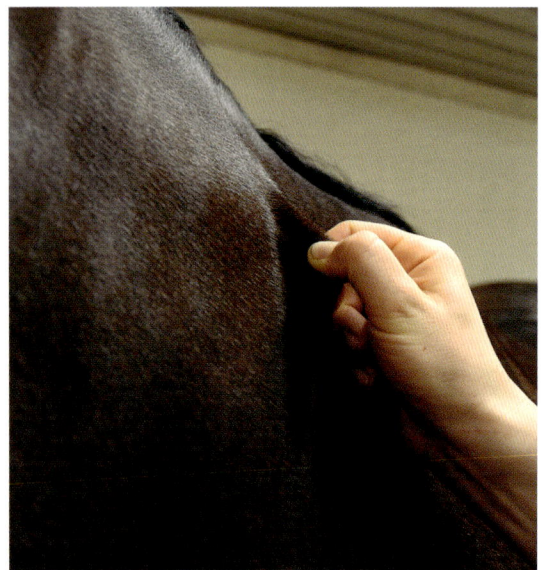 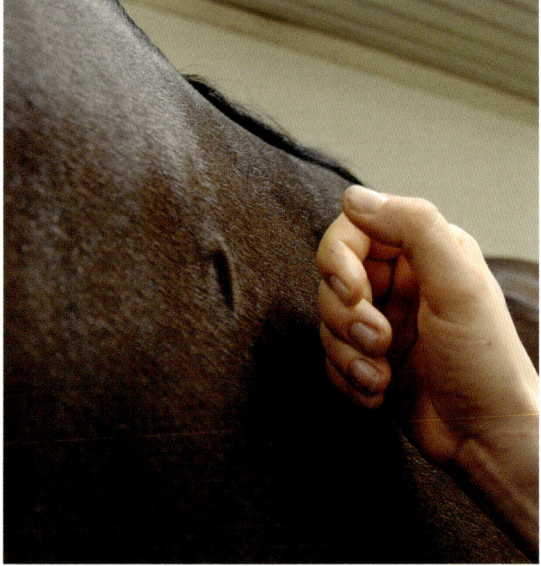

A pinch test can be used to check for dehydration. The skin should return to normal immediately; if it does not return to normal after 2 seconds this may be a sign that the horse is dehydrated.

Other care on overnight stops

Before you turn the horses out, you will need to check them over for any scratches or wounds, as well as places where the tack may have rubbed. Also look for insect bites at this point. Check the state of their feet and shoes – and it is always nice to give them a post-exercise rub (equine physiotherapists can guide you before you go) – but, as a minimum, they should be given a basic brush over.

If the horses have to be stabled overnight it is worth taking them for a graze in hand on a lunge rein so they can have a roll if they want to – but do this before they are brushed!

Dependent on the length of ride, lunchtime or overnight stops will require pre-planning.

Camping

Of course, if you are camping, you will have needed to make arrangements in advance regarding secure turnout for the horses, along with the provision of fodder and hard feed as necessary. You will also have needed to make arrangements for the provision of camping gear for the riders – perhaps including the availability of someone competent to erect tents, and the provision of some kind of toilet facility. Thought should also have been given to comfortable sleeping arrangements compatible with the prevailing weather conditions – if you and your clients are making overnight stops between sustained days of trekking, you will all want a good night's sleep!

Riding Out

If you are to cook around a camp fire, you must first ensure (a) that they are permitted on your intended site/location and (b) that you don't do anything that risks setting fire to an area of open moorland or forest. Regarding food, it is best to have available items that require minimum cooking for suppers around the camp. Although it's true that many people enjoy the idea of producing gourmet meals on a portable grill, in practice, you should decide how much energy you think you'll have for cooking and plan accordingly.

Summary

- Make sure that you ride all the routes that you plan to take clients on in advance and make a note of timings between sections so that you know where you can make up time if you have to.

- Get in touch with local farmers and B&B organisations along your route and plan where you and the horses are going to sleep. Make sure that all the equipment needed for a long ride is in good order and accessible for everyone likely to be leading the rides. Train your horses to graze on a rein and to drink at regular intervals if possible.

TRAINING TIPS

1. Practise riding with all the equipment you need to carry, as this can alter the balance of both horse and rider if you aren't used to it.

2. Investigate options for sections of each route so that you can cut home more quickly if an unforeseen circumstance arises.

3. Make sure that the 'back stop' supporter from the yard and you have a clear way of communicating with each other, and possibly an emergency word for extreme situations!

Chapter 10

Caring for Horses on Return from a Ride

Horses

Caring for tack

Summary

Caring for Horses on Return from a Ride

Taking appropriate care of horses after any ride is a fundamental duty of anyone involved in horse management. However, while the main concern is horse welfare, there are practical benefits for a riding centre, because this is the moment when any problems can be spotted early and treated most time- and cost-effectively. Similarly, basic inspection and cleaning of the tack used will help to maintain it in good order.

Horses

Obviously, the level of care required when you return from a ride will vary according to the length and speed of the ride as well as factors such as the time of the year, temperature and the general fitness of the horses. When you are taking a ride out, always try to walk for the last 10–15 minutes so that all the horses have an opportunity to cool down and allow their pulse rate, respiration rate and body temperature to return to normal. Walking at the end of a ride also serves to allow muscles to relax slowly and dilated blood vessels to slowly return to normal. It also helps in bringing the horses into a state of mental and physical relaxation.

It is useful to be familiar with the resting respiration and pulse rates of the horses you are responsible for. When the horse is at rest, watch his flanks moving in and out as he breathes. Count the in/out movements for 10 seconds. Find the horse's pulse by placing your fingers over the mandibular artery (just inside each branch of the lower jaw). Count the number of beats for 10 seconds. Multiply each of these numbers by 6 to get his respiration and pulse (heart) rates per minute. Although respiration rates vary widely, on average, resting respiration rate is between 8 and 16 per minute and resting pulse rate is about 36 beats per minute. A horse who has worked extremely hard may increase the pulse rate to 140 or more. That rate should drop quickly to about 100 as soon as exercise has stopped and return to the normal rate within 15 minutes. Both respiration and pulse rates should slow significantly during the first few minutes of cooling down.

On return to the yard, the tack should be removed and the horses offered a drink, allowing them to drink as much as they want. When they've finished drinking, on a warm day hose them with cool running water, or sponge liberal amounts of water over their entire body until the water running off is no longer hot. Scrape off any excess water and start hand-walking the horses in a cool, shaded area. (This work should normally be done by centre staff but, if keen clients offer to help, and are competent to do so, their offer can be gratefully accepted.)

If it is hot do not put a sheet or cooler on the horses. Wait until the horses are calm and relaxed before stabling them, and that they are completely cool. It is important to make sure that further water is available – if the horses have worked hard, possibly laced with electrolytes to replace the nutrients and minerals lost through sweating.

The process for cooling horses after a ride in the winter is much the same as it would be any other time of the year. Again it is best to be able to walk the horses for a few minutes at the end of the hack, depending on how long and hard they've been working. This allows the heat generated in the horses' core and muscles to disperse. Keep an eye on respiration rates, as this will give you a guideline as to whether they have recovered. However, on a cold day you might want to cover the horses with moisture-wicking sweat sheets so they don't get chilled by the cold air.

All horses should have their feet picked out – a process that also allows their shoes to be inspected for condition. Legs should be felt to check for any cuts or heat, and a brief inspection made to check that there are no saddle sores or girth galls evident. It may also be prudent to check for signs of any soreness in the mouth, especially if a rider has had problems at the faster gaits, or you saw any evidence of roughness in the way a rider was handling the reins.

Once the horses have been untacked, cooled down and checked for signs of injury, they can be given a brush over and their general management regime resumed in terms of appropriate feeding and watering, turnout, etc.

Caring for tack

When you return from your ride, the tack, as well as the horses, will need to be cared for. Sweaty numnahs will need to be removed and set aside for washing, as will any dirty boots the horse was wearing.

Bits and metalwork can get really grimy, especially after a long ride, so they should be removed from the bridles and soaked in a bucket of hot, soapy water before being rinsed and polished. The bridles should be wiped off with a cloth such as an old flannel or dishcloth dipped in a small bucket of warm water, and thoroughly squeezed out.

After the dirt and grease have been cleaned from the bridles, a coat of saddle soap should be applied with a dry sponge. The soap bar can be dipped into the water to wet it a little but not allowed to lather as it will then leave a white coating on the leather, which may go hard. Alternatively, one of the liquid soaps available can be used.

If the bridles are very greasy or otherwise heavily soiled, a small handful of washing soda crystals added to the water will help enormously, and will not affect the suppleness of the leather.

If you have been caught out in the rain or the tack is particularly muddy, immediate action is required! The bridles should be cleaned as soon as possible, then allowed to dry out very slowly. Do not be tempted to place leatherwork near a heater or a sunny window to speed up the drying process as this will make the leather go very hard – and you may not be able to revive it. When bridles have become very wet, they should be allowed to dry before applying a coat of leather dressing or oil followed by saddle soap.

For saddles, the same method should be used as for bridles, except that it is best to apply the leather dressing or oil only to the flesh side (underneath or rough side) as it soaks in better from this side, and the oil or dressing should not then come off on riders' clothing. Also, some saddle leathers have a coating that will not allow oil to soak in from the grain side (top side).

Saddles should be stored on purpose-made racks, which will not cause indentations on the panel (underside) of the saddle, and will allow the air to circulate around it. Girths, if they are made of leather, should be treated in the same way. If they are neoprene or fabric, they can be placed in the washing machine inside a pillowcase on a cool wash with non-biological detergent.

Summary

- Always plan your ride so that there is time and suitable terrain to walk gently for the last mile or so to allow the horses (and riders) to relax and stretch their muscles. If you have a large ride and the weather is warm, make sure that the yard staff are waiting to help you sponge off the horses on your return.

- Make sure that tack is sponged off and cleaned as soon as possible so that it remains in good condition and does not cause sores.

TRAINING TIPS

1. Acclimatise the horses in your care to being washed or hosed off with the minimum of fuss. This may be a time-consuming process initially, but start gently with their feet, work up the legs and on to the body. They will become used to it eventually!

2. Have a system for 'stripping' the tack (taking it apart) so that you don't get pieces from one bridle mixed with another.

3. Have a yard policy in place for feeding and hydrating the horses on return from a long ride and make sure everyone abides by it.

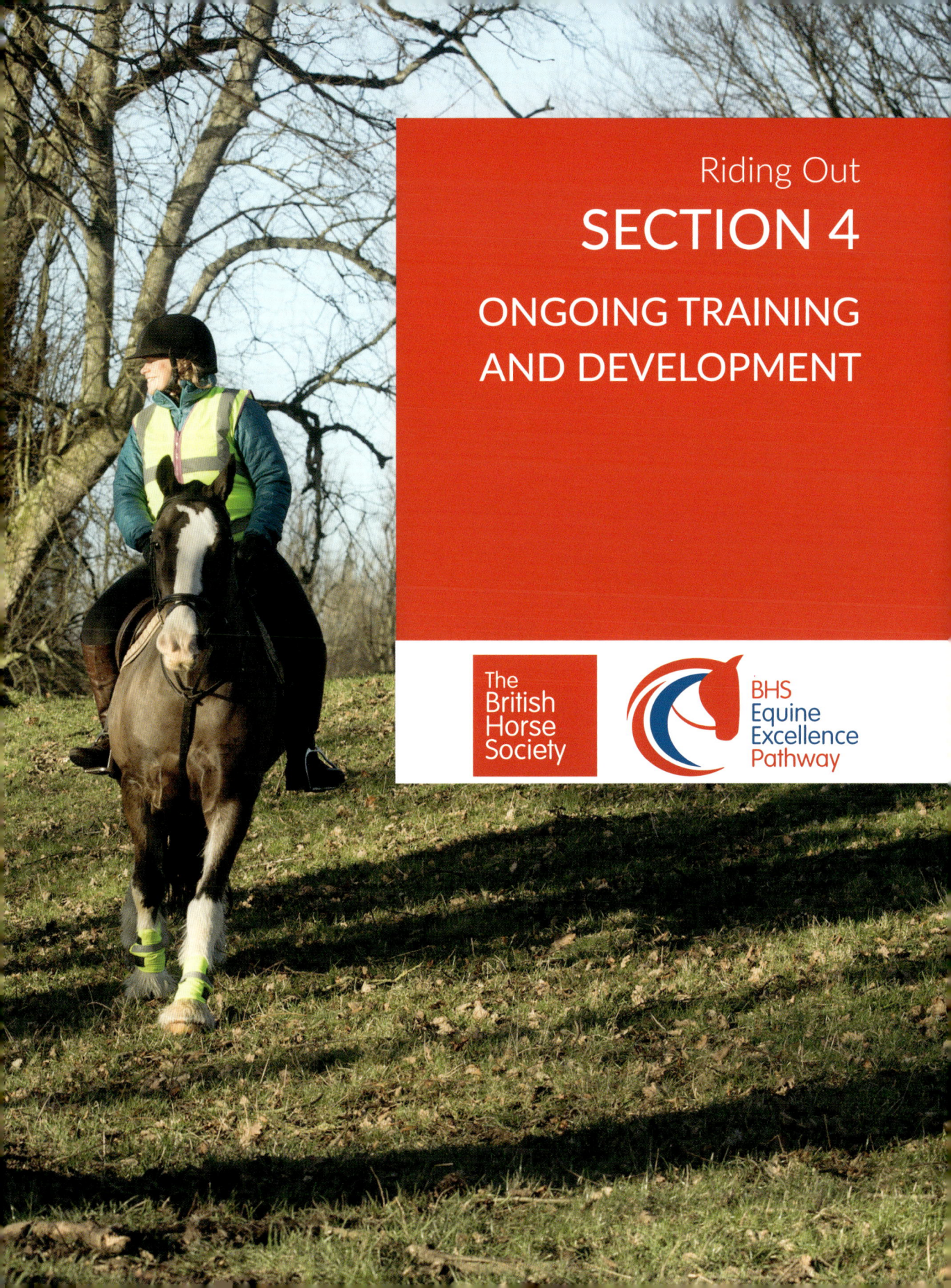

Chapter 11

Staff Training and Development

Training policy

Interpersonal skills – communication

Self-reflection

Summary

Staff Training and Development

The owner of a riding centre will have responsibility for the management and training of staff at the yard and, even if not actually the owner, a Stage 3 Trail Leader will have some responsibility for these issues.

Training policy

It is a legal requirement that there must be a written training policy in place for all staff, which must include:

- An annual appraisal.

- Planned continued professional development based on recognition of any gaps in knowledge or skill.

- Use of online courses and literature.

If no staff are employed by the centre, the holder of the centre's licence must demonstrate their own development plans, and evidence of attendance at the specified CPD (Continuing Personal Development) training on a regular basis must be provided.

All records of staff appraisals, CPD and correspondence must be available to an inspector and kept for at least 3 years, beginning with the date on which the record was created.

New staff should go through an induction period. This should include being given details on their job role and specification. In other words, they will need to be told all the things they will have to do. Where there are gaps in their experience, knowledge and skill, training will have to be provided and ideally recorded. All staff should have an annual appraisal intended to increase motivation, making sure that everyone on the yard is kept updated with the latest developments and can 'buy into' improving the business.

If staff are to be suitably prepared for the work they are being asked to do this will often mean that they have to be trained in specific areas. In every business now, all staff have to understand the requirements for Health and Safety, Safeguarding, Equality and Diversity and Data Protection. Another requirement which, while not 'statutory' still makes good business sense, is that of 'customer service'.

Health and safety

As stated earlier in Chapters 3 and 4, riding establishments that provide hacking or instruction to clients usually employ Ride Leaders, coaches and other staff to help with the day-to-day running of the yard. In these businesses, the Health and Safety at Work Act 1974 is applicable, and section 2 of the Act states: *'It shall be the duty of every employer to ensure, so far as is reasonably practicable, the health, safety and welfare at work of all his employees.'*

However, employees also have responsibilities under various elements of legislation. For example, they must attend health and safety training sessions, wear any personal protective equipment provided and abide by the safety management system rules that have been put in place.

Safeguarding

The aims of a safeguarding policy were explained earlier in Chapter 4. Staff working with young people should have undergone a DBS check (or national equivalent), and should be trained to understand their roles in the safeguarding process. Key elements of this are:

- To ensure robust safeguarding arrangements and procedures are in operation to provide children and young people with appropriate safety and protection.

- To take all reasonable, practical steps to protect children from harm, discrimination and degrading treatment and to respect their rights, wishes and feelings.

- To ensure that everyone else involved understands their roles and responsibilities in respect of safeguarding.

- To engage with appropriate learning opportunities to recognise, identify and respond to signs of abuse, neglect and other safeguarding concerns relating to children and young people.

- To ensure appropriate action is taken in the event of incidents/concerns of abuse and to support the individual(s) who raise or disclose the concern. All concerns or allegations of poor practice or abuse are to be taken seriously and responded to swiftly and appropriately.

- To ensure that confidential, detailed and accurate records of all safeguarding concerns are maintained and stored securely. (*See also* Data Protection, below.)

- To maintain high standards of behaviour and good practice through compliance with BEF codes of conduct produced for instructors, coaches, parents/guardians, junior members and volunteers.

Equality and diversity

Equality and diversity means that no one who comes into contact with anyone at your centre should be discriminated against on the grounds of age, gender, disability, race, language, ethnic origin, nationality, colour, parental or marital status, pregnancy, religious belief, class or social background, sexual orientation, gender reassignment or political belief.

All reasonable steps should be taken to ensure that everyone who wishes to join in the equestrian activities at your centre should be treated fairly.

Data protection – GDPR

The requirements of a business under the General Data Protection Regulation (GDPR) were explained in Chapter 4. Key points in terms of staff training are that 'data' refers to *any* personal information stored, and the requirements of GDPR apply to *anyone* involved in data storage or processing. They could, therefore, apply to anyone within the centre who is ever involved in what might be termed, even loosely, as a 'secretarial' role. This could include such matters as keeping contact details of clients or suppliers of services, so it is important that any such staff receive appropriate training in the matter of compliance.

Staff training.

Customer service

In the equestrian world, there are aspects of customer service that could equally well be presented as 'customer care' – as can be seen in conjunction to issues such as safeguarding and health and safety concerns.

In more general terms, the concept of 'customer service' can be seen in the way that staff relate to clients, and a very important start for staff training is for them to recognise the importance of dealing with clients. The smiling face and 'Good morning, can I help you?' go a long way to providing clients with a satisfying experience. In this respect, it is best for the owner to lead by example and always be pleasant and offer a 'Good morning', checking that the staff know what they are doing for the day ahead.

Taking the time to explain what is going on to riders is always worthwhile. Likewise, keeping staff informed as to the daily yard routines and trained to deal with all eventualities will have a positive effect when dealing with clients.

It is essential that staff understand the importance of maintaining a dialogue with clients when riding out. Keeping a focus and assessing how clients are coping with the ride and their horses is very important. Knowing when to give riders help is often crucial to keeping the ride safe.

Interpersonal skills – communication

Communication is part and parcel of the customer service just mentioned, and lies at the heart of everything in a client-facing industry such as a commercial riding establishment. However, it is also key to effective interaction between everyone who works at the riding centre and, indeed, with people who provide services to the business. Although the examples given in the text below 'follow on' from the issue of customer service and interaction with clients, they are relevant to all communication.

Communication is a two-way process where active listening plays as important a role as speaking fluently. Speaking fluently without listening will make any conversation a very short-lived one.

It is particularly important when you are taking out relatively inexperienced riders who may be nervous and out of their comfort zone. Good communication helps clients feel at ease and comfortable in what may be a somewhat alien environment, and will reduce their anxiety and build their confidence.

Communication methods

Communication is about much more than actual words. The tone of voice, the attention to what the other person is saying, the messages given through body language and the accuracy and clarity of what we say are also key elements of good communication.

Listening

Listening is a really important skill and involves not only picking up sound waves but understanding the meaning of words so that you can analyse them, interpret them, and act accordingly. In addition to that, it helps you to communicate more successfully and build a receptive, cooperative relationship with the other person.

To engage in a two-way conversation with clients, you will have to ask them questions about their riding experience (if any) and their goals for their ride out with you on a particular day.

Questions can be broadly classified under two categories:

1. **Open questions.** These questions are also known as the 'Wh-' questions as they are usually preceded by 'Who', 'When', 'Where', 'What' and 'Why'. When people answer these types of questions, they tend to focus more on giving descriptive answers.

    Example: 'What experience have you had riding outside?'

2. **Closed questions.** These questions can be easily answered in a few words, even with a simple 'Yes' or 'No'. They are asked to get a quick response from the listener about facts and figures. The listener tends to put more stress on their memory as compared to processing thoughts while answering these questions.

    Example: 'Are you comfortable cantering across a field?'

Body language

Body language can say a great deal more than the words you may use. The purpose of communication is to engage the people you are talking to. There are three main types of body language that you need to consider when dealing with others, whether it is clients, staff or visiting professionals.

Eye contact

Eye contact is essential. If you want someone to listen then you need to look at them – not for too long, of course, but enough to show you are addressing them and that they might want to listen. If you are in a one-to-one situation, such as assessing a new client or taking a booking, you may need to look away every now and again as staring at one person without a break can be a little unnerving for the recipient!

If you are talking to a group of people, perhaps briefing them about your forthcoming ride, then you should aim to make eye contact with as many people as possible. Don't stare at anyone in particular, just keep moving to each individual and try to hold their gaze for a moment.

Finally, it is really important that you look at people when they ask you questions and you should give a direct reply when you answer.

Body position

You can tell by looking at someone whether they are excited, bored, relaxed or stressed. If their shoulders are slumped, their head hanging down or their arms and legs are tightly crossed it sends a message about how they are feeling.

To get someone interested in what you're saying you need to look interested yourself. So if you're sitting down, you be should leaning forward with your arms open and not crossed. Crossing your arms looks defensive (as if you are worried or scared about something).

If you're standing up you will need to hold your head up and have your arms open – that way you can get the final aspects of body language right.

Gesture and movement

If you watch a television conversation with the sound off, you will notice people's gestures as they talk. How people sit or stand is noticeable, but what really emphasises face-to-face conversation is how people use their expressions, heads, hands and shoulders to make a point or emphasise words. Gestures bring life to a conversation.

- ◊ Spread arms can express the size of an idea or object.

- ◊ A closed fist can express strength or anger.

- ◊ An open palm can ask for calm (if the hand is raised) or appeal to reason (with fingers pointing down).

- ◊ Moving the whole body can express energy or urgency.

Spoken language

A major part of communicating successfully with others depends on the style and language that you use in your communication. If you are talking to clients you haven't met before and are explaining the basic procedures you will be following while hacking out, you won't use the same kind of language that you would when you are training staff to ride and lead for example.

What you say, combined with the way you say it, determines how the listeners perceive your message. There may be times when it is important that you are firm from a safety aspect, and times when you need to be friendly and supportive if a rider is nervous or unsure. In all situations, though, you should keep listening intently and empathise whenever needed.

Sometimes you may have to deal with complaints or concerns from your clients and, in this situation, it is important that you remain patient and try to understand the situation and listen to the other person's point of view before trying to solve the problem.

Being able to understand and work with others in teams or groups is another important aspect of using interpersonal skills.

Self-reflection

This is about reflecting on your own performance, evaluating it honestly and discovering ways to improve it through skills development, and is relevant to everyone in the business from the owner/manager to the most junior Ride Helper.

Self-reflection may require you to work with others to identify your strengths and weaknesses, find out what support and progression may be available to help you develop a plan covering your personal and professional goals, and then put that plan into action.

Evaluating your own performance can help improve your self-confidence, motivation and morale and help you to understand any future career steps. When you evaluate the way you managed any given task, whether it is assessing riders, taking a ride out, or a management task on the yard, it is important to break down each task and consider honestly how well you performed.

For example, as a Ride Leader, when you have returned from a ride, it is useful to reflect on what went well and any areas that you would like to improve for the next time. Ask yourself if you have been able to manage your time effectively, making sure that you got the ride out on time, dealing with any unexpected developments on route and showing flexibility if things don't go quite as you hoped for. You will also have to reflect on the suitability of the horses used for riding out and their basic way of going. For example, is it time that you arranged more training for them on a particular aspect or improved their general level of fitness?

In trying to identify your main strengths as a Ride Leader, it is always useful to ask others for feedback and compare this to your own judgement (in fact, dialogue with other people may also mean that you will be able to help others in your yard regarding certain aspects of the work, or it may open a new doorway to further career progression). If you consider that there are any gaps between expected and required performance and actual performance, then you will need to take action to address them. You may need to seek help for training to improve your skills and knowledge and you must consider the best way to address this. Ask yourself whether you are taking advantage of opportunities to increase your self-confidence and learn from new experiences. Consider any areas that you find more challenging and how you will improve on these in the future. For the role of Ride Leader, communication skills are paramount and it is not always easy to retain professional standards and a pleasant demeanour if you are dealing with a difficult client or a very nervous rider. Think about how you might deal with a particular situation more positively in future and, if necessary, what help you may need to improve.

Self-management skills are also very important, as you will spend a lot of time away from the yard in charge of other people and horses, and you must be absolutely trustworthy and reliable in this role.

Summary

- It is crucial that every yard and trekking centre has policies that cover all the topics mentioned above. These must be kept safely and must be instantly accessible for any official who requests access to them, but they must also be secured so that they cannot be accessed by unauthorised people, as they will contain sensitive personal data that can only be shared under certain conditions with certain people.

- Customer service is the lynchpin for successful recreational riding establishments and it is worth investing in training for all staff in this area.

TRAINING TIPS

1. Self-reflection is a useful technique for improving the way you carry out tasks, and will save you time and energy in the long run – as long as you are honest with yourself! It is very important that you develop the skill of being able to assess the way you have done something and analyse any opportunities for doing it better next time. It can also highlight when you have done something well so you can refer back to it for the future.

2. When you are reflecting on a certain experience or exercise that you have completed, consider the following:

    » *Describe the experience*

    What happened? When and where did the exercise take place? Any other thoughts about the situation?

    » *Reflect*

    How did you manage the situation? What thoughts did you have? How did you feel while you were doing it? Were there factors that influenced the situation? What have you learned from the experience?

    » *Theory*

    Was the outcome of the exercise just as you expected or did something occur that you hadn't planned for? Do you think, if you had acted differently, the outcome might have altered? What might you do differently next time?

What's Next?

What's Next?

The British Horse Society Ride Leader Pathway has been created to encourage and support riders and yard staff, from those helping and assisting at riding schools and trekking centres through to experienced Ride Leaders who will be able to confidently take out long distance, overnight treks. The benefits of riding out of the arena have been pointed out throughout this book, but the value of being experienced and qualified in this field cannot be overemphasised. As a Ride Leader, you will be able to empower people to socialise with other horse lovers, to observe nature while safely exploring new terrain, to improve their equestrian abilities and build their confidence.

BHS Ride Leader Pathway (in Complete Horsemanship)

Career pathway	What qualifications do I need to study?	
BHS Stage 1	Stage 1 Care	+ Stage 1 Ride *
BHS Stage 2 Ride Leader	Stage 2 Care	+ Stage 2 Riding Out
BHS Stage 3 Trail Leader	Stage 3 Care	+ Stage 3 Riding Out
BHS Stage 4 Senior Trail Yard Manager	Stage 4 Care	+ Stage 4 Management
BHS Stage 5 Performance Trail Centre Manager	Stage 5 Care	+ Stage 5 Management

* Taken in conjunction with the **Ride Safe Award**.